H◆PE
LESSONS FROM A
HUMMINGBIRD

ISBN: 1-4392-2136-7
ISBN-13: 9781439221365

Cover Design By: Kelly Trujillo at .simplbydesign@cox.net?
Author Photo By: Nan Cuccia

Visit www.booksurge.com to order additional copies.

HOPE

LESSONS FROM A HUMMINGBIRD

A Redemptive Adventure
of how a regular guy got free
from depression and rage

WILLIAM M. CUCCIA

Table of Contents

———◆———

Therefore, there is now no condemnation for those who are in Christ Jesus, because through Christ Jesus the law of the Spirit of life set me free from the law of sin and death.

— Romans 8:1–2

Dedication

This book is dedicated to the glory of God.
Truly my life has become an open book so that others can experience the healing presence and power of deliverance that God still offers today. You are my Light in Darkness.

My wife Nan, thanks for the example you've been to me of the power of God's forgiveness. Words can't express the admiration I have for you. Your trust in God and "BIG" faith has been an incredible example to me. Finally, thanks for believing in Hope. Welcome home, Nan Cuccia, Welcome home.

My buddy Evan, your faithful friendship has been an example of loyalty to me. Thanks for being such a great listener. That's right, a great listener. Your example of hard work is an inspiration to me.

Kirk, your counsel and mentorship proved timely and allowed me to become a "regular guy." Thanks.

Doug, I will always be indebted to you for your willingness to come and pray with me on that Friday morning June 13th. Your faithfulness to the King of Kings is truly remarkable.

Introduction:

A Hummingbird Named Hope

IT'S SUNDAY MORNING; my wife Nancy and I are about to hand over a baby hummingbird to a lady who releases hummingbirds.

A week ago, Nan and I were in the backyard of a house we were thinking about buying in San Juan Capistrano, California. As we sat down on the stone planter as the sun radiated through the trees above our heads, Nan pointed to a place in the lawn where there were these two little eyes peering up at us from between some leaves. My first thought was, *how did I not step on that little thing?* I guess maybe that's because most of my life I've stepped on people, opportunity, and blessing, then just moved on without any remorse or thought.

Nan decided she wanted to figure out a way to take this little bird home with us and nurture it until we could find it proper care. My wife has a real heart for animals; she said, "Let's figure out a way to take this little bird home with us." This little bird I've affectionately named *Hope*—hope that just maybe we could take care of this little guy and help it live.

The longest recorded lifespan of a hummingbird is a female Broad-tailed Hummingbird that was tagged then recaptured twelve years later, making her at least twelve years old. Hummingbirds are the tiniest and most fascinating of birds. The early Spanish explorers called them *Joyas Volardores,* or flying jewels.

Here are a few interesting facts about hummingbirds that I'll address in detail throughout this book, along with the lessons I've learned. Hummingbirds are built for power and dazzle. They are little more than flight muscles covered with feathers. Thirty percent of a hummingbird's weight consists of flight muscles. The hummingbird's tiny brain, 4.2% of its body weight, is proportionately the largest in the bird kingdom. So what I surmise from these two interesting facts is that hummingbirds are strong and smart. What better creature to learn lessons from?

A hummingbird's flight speed can average 25–30 mph, and they can dive up to 60 mph. In their non-stop quest for fuel, hummingbirds may visit upwards of 2,000 flowers per day. So these little creatures spend a lot of energy getting fed. When they find what they're looking for, they can get to it fast.

As I studied that helpless little creature stuck in the grass, I never would have thought it had so much potential. People are no different. My problem has always been that I can't see over the blades of grass to see what's out there for me.

As I walked from the backyard out to the street where our car was parked, my thoughts drifted to what was going to happen to Nan and me. Would we stay married, or was Nan going to leave me and start a new life? I still had so many unanswered questions about where our marriage was headed. When I got to my car, I found a plastic water bottle. In the back of my car was a razor blade cutter that I had just bought a couple of days before to clean some glass at my office. I had thought about throwing the razor blade away the day I used it at my office, but for some reason I hung onto it. I had thrown it in the back of my car, not really thinking any more about it.

Now, I cut the top of the plastic bottle off and used it to scoop Hope into the bottom of the water bottle. I then covered the top with the lid I had cut. In retrospect, having the razor blade made it easier to transport the little hummingbird. At fifty-two years old, I've found that there's little in life that's left to chance.

During the entire drive home, which was about thirteen miles, Nan held onto the bottle to keep it from rattling around in the car. Each time I glanced at the little hummingbird in the bottle, I wondered if she would even make it until we got home. It was a typical Southern California Summer afternoon—hot. I didn't know if we should turn the air conditioning full blast or keep the temperature warm for Hope.

With every bump in the road Nan and I would look at Hope in the bottle, then glance at each other with confirmation that we both thought it was still alive. The drive seemed longer than normal as we waited for some type of movement from Hope to acknowledge that she was okay. She seemed like she may be struggling to stay alive. I had the thought that maybe she wasn't getting enough air, so I suggested that Nan remove the lid I had made to let more air in.

Once we arrived at home, we pulled into the garage and my eyes made contact with this antique birdcage we had bought a few years before for our little finch Francisco. Francisco had outgrown the cage, but we held onto it because it was an antique. The cage had just sat on a shelf in our garage and collected dust over the years. I got the cage down, took it out in our backyard and hosed it down with some water. Once I dried it off, I brought the cage upstairs to our bedroom where Nan had kept watch over Hope. I think Nan was just checking to see if our new little bird "project" was still breathing.

Nan prepared the cage with some paper towels, some brush we picked up from the yard, and some cotton balls to make a soft place for Hope to rest. Nan has a way with animals. She was raised on a farm in Kentucky and learned to care for animals from her father at an early age. She would have made a great veterinarian. Nan displayed great care as she transferred Hope from the bottle to her new cage. Once in the cage, the bird remained motionless.

We had stopped at a local pet store on our way home to ask if they knew how to care for a hummingbird. There were a couple of young teenagers who were working the checkout counters, and even though they thought Hope was adorable, they didn't have a clue what to do other than to try to feed her with sugar water through a dropper. So our next stop was to Rite Aid to pick up an eyedropper to feed her. Nan filled up the eyedropper with red sugar water from the pet store and tried to get Hope to respond to the dropper. She would put the end of the dropper up to Hope's beak but could get no response. After a half hour or so of failed attempts, Nan squealed out, "She's eating!" I ran into the bedroom and watched the joy on my wife's face as little Hope sucked the artificial nectar from the dropper.

For the next week, we fed Hope with a dropper filled with sugar water, crushed worms (for protein), and a supplement for birds called "super preen" (amino acids). Hummingbirds have to eat every four hours or they can die. Their little heart beats at a rate of 1,260 beats per minute.

When they are forced to go without food for extended periods of time, they go into a state called "torpor." In torpor, the metabolism slows down, saving up to sixty percent of the bird's available energy (this usually happens at night).

All in all, these little creations are very needy. A real lesson for me was to see just how patient God is with me. I had the thought more than once in that week that if Hope needed this much care and nurturing, how much do I need from my heavenly Father? Webster's online dictionary says that to *nurture* means, "to care for and encourage the growth of." That's a very powerful word. Think about having the ability to nurture someone or something so that it can grow and take care of itself and become something great.

Webster's online dictionary says that to nurture means, **"to care for and encourage the growth of."**

The thought of that little hummingbird being able to take flight and have the freedom to live life the way she was created was so exciting. What a wonderful opportunity to be part of Hope's nurturing process. We have power to nurture or to destroy the relationships that come our way. In this book, I'll share with you some of what I've learned about both.

I have a greater understanding of the joy that God experiences from meeting our needs. I actually began to look forward to feeding Hope and learning ways to meet this hummingbird's needs. When I did something to take care of one of Hope's needs, it brought me joy.

So many times over that week as I was alone with Hope feeding her or just watching her move around her cage, I thought about how lucky I've been in life to live in safety and have my needs met. I also thought about the less fortunate who live in places around the world where danger is just a part of their day, along with hunger and lack of shelter. I had took a good look in the mirror and realized that life is much better than I ever thought.

I used to think that I was bothering God with what I perceived to be important needs, and I struggle with the lie that God really doesn't care about my needs. The truth is, God delights in meeting my needs. God created us to meet a need that He had; it's called relationship.

In any relationship I've ever been involved in, the greatest joy is from giving to the other person. Meeting needs is a blessing. God finds joy in taking care of our needs. Wow, think about that! The Bible says it this way: "...casting all your cares upon Him for He cares for you" (1 Peter 5:7). Watching Hope made me realize that God does care.

We had the pleasure of seeing Hope go from just sitting in her cage motionless, to moving ever so slowly on her weak little legs, to hovering all over her cage, to flying back and forth from branch to branch in her cage. This all happened in just one short week, I would've thought it would have taken weeks before Hope could fly. I'm really good at assessing situations with great authority *and* confidence and coming up with the absolute wrong analysis. I've been groomed my entire life to make prideful wrong decisions and destroy everything in my path with those decisions. That's what rage, anger, and sheer stupidity does.

Nan and I just found out that today (remember it was Sunday) that if we had kept Hope in her cage much longer, she would probably have ended up breaking her wings and dying. When people are left alone too long in cages, whatever cage has them imprisoned, people lose their way. There's so much truth in what I learned that week from caring for this little hummingbird.

In seven short days, I was challenged with a lifetime of lessons that I'm passing on to you. These are lessons that can change a person's life if they let them. I know these "hummingbird lessons" can "nurture" (build up and encourage growth in) a soul. That's my hope for everyone who reads this book.

It's said that it's better to learn from others' mistakes. Well, this story tells of a lifetime of mistakes—but also of my learning.

Prologue:

A Redemptive Adventure

He has sent redemption to His people. He has ordained His covenant forever. His name is holy and awe-inspiring.

— Psalm 111:9

NAN AND I are waiting for a call from Lisa Birkle, Assistant Director of the Wetlands Bird Estuary. We're going to give Hope to her so she can properly release the bird. See, there are things that Hope needs that we can't provide for her, so we're going to give her to an authority on raising and releasing hummingbirds. What's interesting is we didn't just decide to call Lisa and ask her to take Hope and care for her. No, we prayed that we would be led to the right person today, because Nan had some concerns about what to do next. So Nan "surfed the 'Net" and found the name of an expert in caring for and releasing hummingbirds.

This woman put Nan in touch with the Lisa to whom we're going to give Hope, who happens to be going to a church this morning that is less than two minutes from our home in Rancho Santa Margarita. And, it's the first time that this woman is going to that church location. What are the chances of that happening? I choose to believe that God has His hand all over this situation. God cares for this little bird more than Nan and I do.

So many times I've thought that circumstances are just that—circumstances. I'm learning instead that God is sovereign, and He's working behind the scenes on our behalf. Think about it. If God is leading Nancy and me to care for this little hummingbird so that we'll nurture her along and get her to the next place where she can prepare to be free, how much more is God working for us? "God does work all things together for good to those who are called according to his purposes" (Romans 8:28).

This is the same journey that God has me on right now as well. Though it's sometimes painful, it's exciting to learn how to trust God with my life. I'm on a parallel journey with Hope. This book is about how God set me free from the destruction of rage, and how He put my life back together. Join me in this redemptive adventure.

This book is a message of hope. Hope for today. There is hope. The lessons in this book will leave you with *principles of hope* that can change your life if you practice them. God is in the business of taking lives that have been destroyed and healing them so they can live life in freedom without guilt, shame, or bitter resentment keeping them bound. I call this "the great work of redemption," and it's an adventure.

This book is a message of hope. Hope for today. There is hope. The lessons in this book will leave you with principles of hope that can change your life if you practice them.

Just as Hope has hit the ceiling in her cage and needs help to be freed to fly unencumbered. I too hit the ceiling of my "cage" and came crashing down with broken wings and no strength to go on.

Sometimes perseverance can be a detriment. For years I was able to live life with my own strength and not depend upon God to see me through. It took a long time, and I do mean a long time, but I finally came crashing down. I became malnourished; my immune system was compromised to the point that I was suffering from boils on my body. One on my arm in particular became so infected that I had to go to the emergency room to have surgery.

I finally got to the point that I just couldn't do life one more day. I had to reach out whether I wanted to or not. I didn't have the physical or emotional strength to go on. I could not do it myself. I woke up one morning and asked Nan to call a pastor friend of ours. He was gracious enough to come over and pray with me that morning. I don't remember what he prayed, but there was life in his prayers. The Spirit of God began a work in my life that He's continuing daily.

By the way, we made it to the church on time. We met Lisa who is going to release Hope. I was able to take a few photos of Nan giving Hope to Lisa. As I clicked off a few pictures, I wondered if we would ever see Hope again. Probably not, but I knew one thing for sure. I would never forget these last eight days. I won't ever forget what Hope's eyes looked like the first time we saw her caught in the grass.

I won't ever forget the lessons that I have learned from taking care of a hummingbird named Hope.

Lesson 1:

Mistakes

Most hummingbirds unfortunately die during their first year, but those that do survive that first year have an average life span of three to four years.

FORTUNATELY, THIS MISTAKE didn't cost me my life, but it could have. Our mistakes become God's greatest works of redemption.

In 1994, my wife Nancy was given an incredible gift from God that most all women would love to have. No, I'm not the incredible gift that God gave to Nan. We do have a wonderful story of how God brought us together in 1991, and I'll share that story later on.

Years before Nan had received this gift she had signed over a beautiful home in Laguna Beach, California, to her former husband. He was much older than she was, and she felt that it was the right thing to do at the time. In February 1994, Nan ran across a historical home in San Juan Capistrano, and I've always known in my heart that this was God's way of redeeming and restoring the loss of what Nan had given away years before.

We had just put down a non-refundable deposit on a new home that was going to be completed in about four months. We were excited about moving into a home where we could choose the appliances and cabinets, flooring and all the stuff you get to choose when you purchase a newly built home.

I personally was excited that everything in the house would be efficient and new. We were living in San Clemente in a beautiful Spanish home that was built in 1926. Though it was beautiful, not everything worked and we were constantly putting money and sweat equity into the house to make it more efficient.

Everything was moving along quite well, until Nan took a drive one day into a historic neighborhood and found her incredible gift—a historical Spanish hacienda with courtyards, dark rough-sawn beams in the living room, dark wood floors and Spanish pavers. It was truly a beautiful home in a beautiful setting. And get this: it had a "for sale" sign in the front yard.

Nan called me right away, and we went to see the house together. When we called on the house, we found out from the agent that the home had just been leased the day before.

One thing I really love about my wife is she doesn't take no for an answer. She doesn't quit easily. We asked the agent if the owner wouldn't rather sell the house than lease it. Her response was, "Well, probably. Let me call him and I'll get back to you." We were both so excited and anxious.

A few days later on a Saturday morning, we drove up to the house on a whim to look at it again. As we approached the house, a man in a van drove up and parked ahead of us. Nan and I looked at each other and didn't even have to say anything. We both knew this man was the owner.

We approached his van and introduced ourselves as the couple that had called about buying his house. His response was puzzling to us. "What do you mean?" he said. He was there to get the house ready for the people who were going to lease the home. The agent had leased the house to a friend and had not even mentioned us to the owner. I said, "Well, wouldn't you rather sell the house?" His response was yes, but he needed to speak with the agent about the lease.

We were able to get our "non-refundable" deposit back on the new home (without this money we would not have been able to buy Nan's dream house on the hill). By the way, the agent who had the listing told us "the developer had never done that before." The owner of our new Spanish hacienda on the hill was able to get out of the lease agreement, and *voila,* Nan had an incredible gift from her heavenly Father.

God is good, and He loves to give gifts to His children. The home we moved into was Nan's dream come true. It was the home I believe she saw us growing old in, entertaining friends and family. We put our footprints on that home during the six years that we lived there. We buried both of her parent's ashes in the yard of that home. Though our time spent there was not what Nan hoped, we still made a mark on that land.

This was not just any home. It rested at the top of a hill that overlooked the Mission of San Juan Capistrano and had wonderful views of Dana Point harbor. We could hear the bells chime from the mission and the whistle of the trains when they'd stop in town. The view to the northeast would be painted with incredible rainbows from time to time, even double rainbows on some occasions. Hawks would fly over our property on a regular basis. This was the home that God had provided for us. It was a romantic home that Nan named *"Casa Luna,"* house of the moon, because at night the moon would shine directly down and light up our courtyard, which was wrapped on three sides by our house.

Little did I know that later forcing her to sell this home would bring so much destruction to our marriage. At that time I didn't understand how important a home and roots are to a woman. It's as important as my career and call is to me. It was a painful mistake that I've had to release to God and hope that someday both Nan and I can be completely free of the pain and embrace our future. I forced Nan into selling the house because I had given into the fear that we would not be able to afford to stay there. I didn't believe that God could provide for us. I caused Nan's dream to be short lived and her life to be a nightmare for many years. This was a big mistake but it wasn't the biggest mistake I'd make.

There are so many mistakes I've made that I can share that illustrate how rage can defeat a person and cause decisions to be made that are painfully regretted. This mistake destroyed my marriage for many years and could have been the death of a union that God had ordained. All around us we see marriages being torn apart at such a fierce rate that it's frightening. To think that I made such a huge mistake and that God is big enough to make something beautiful out of such a disastrous decision, or series of decisions, is beyond my comprehension.

I first became aware that something was seriously wrong with the way I responded to life when Nan and I were returning home from a ministry trip in Japan. I was overcome with a black depression that hit me with such a sudden viciousness that I remember the exact moment. I was on the plane coming back from a wonderful ministry trip in Japan.

After falling in love with a culture and people that I previously had so many prejudices toward, I was caught up in my thoughts about how wonderful the Japanese people are and what great new friends we had made. In a moment, and I mean a moment, I was overwhelmed with the thought that I was soon going to be back home in the same old rut of life.

Darkness suddenly surrounded me. This black depression lasted for eight straight days. At night the depression became terror. Fear kept me awake for almost the entire eight days and nights. The only relief I would get is when I would pick up my guitar and sing worship songs. I would go out into our garage and just play until the sun came up. Then I would sleep for a few hours before I would begin another day of torment.

Again, this was the first time I became aware of the depression and torment that would accompany it. For years depression would come in seasons of my life, followed by tormenting thoughts of self-hatred, defeat, and anger. This depression would be initiated by the emotion of fear and many times manifest itself with rage towards those I loved the most.

I believed the lie that this was just the way people deal with the issues that present themselves to us as we walk through life. I knew nothing of the liberty that comes when we receive Christ into our lives as Savior and Lord. I knew I was saved, but I was living in constant defeat. Victory seemed unobtainable.

Nan and I have talked several times over the years about the depression, self-hatred, and rage. Our discussions for years ended up in outbursts of rage on my part. Why couldn't Nan understand that I didn't have the power to choose to not get down and then have the depression rear its ugly head as rage? I know now that maybe she will never understand, and that's okay.

Looking back on that trip to Japan, Nan realized as a result of her own study as an herbalist that the diet in Japan and the lengthy trip played a role in this manic episode. The high salt diet and the change in time zones played a major part in my depression episode. I share this because many times what contributes to depression is more than just emotions.

As the time in San Juan Capistrano passed, the rage and depression episodes escalated, I began to destroy other relationships within the church where I was the pastor. The church we had started in 1994 had grown within the first twenty-four months to a nice congregation of 200 plus members (as pastors count their sheep, that included men, women, children and on occasion any pets or animals that might find their way into the community center where we were meeting in Dana Point).

One morning while I was giving one of my "God-inspired, life-changing messages" a ferret ran across the auditorium and caused quite a stir. I was excited because that was one more head to count for that Sunday service. Jesus always counted just the men, like when he fed the 5,000. Estimates with the women and children made it closer to twelve to fifteen thousand. I guess that's one of the major differences between Jesus and the modern-day pastor, or at least this pastor.

As I began to go deeper and deeper into the darkness of the rage and depression, I began to speak some pretty powerful self-fulfilling prophesies over the church, myself, and my wife. "I'll never be able to take the church to the next level." "Maybe my job was to just start the church and someone else needs to take over." I was bound by a fear that paralyzed me. I succumbed to the fear instead of trusting God.

The next thing I knew I was constantly bombarding my family and myself with negative smut that would eventually bring the church, my home, and myself to a crashing halt. It was just part of the destructive pattern of isolation that I learned at an early age. Fear was instilled in me at an early age and the fear would cause me to isolate.

> I was bound by a fear that paralyzed me. I succumbed to the fear instead of trusting God.

Finally one Sunday morning in June 2000, I told my wife I couldn't pastor any longer and just wrote a letter of resignation. I didn't really seek any counsel. I just made a compulsive decision to leave and isolate myself from everyone and anyone. I remember that Sunday morning going out into my yard and planting a tree. I felt free again. This freedom would be fleeting.

What I didn't realize was that fleeing and isolating was the unhealthiest thing I could do to myself—and to everyone else in my life as well. What a mistake that was. But it wasn't the biggest mistake. No, the biggest mistake was yet to come.

For about two months I felt an absence from the darkness of depression and rage. At one point, about ten months after I left the church, I spent thirty-eight days locked up in one of our bedrooms. Day after day I would just play solitaire on my computer and would not speak to anyone including my wife. I was doing the only thing I had known to do, isolate and be alone. What I didn't realize at the time was that isolation just brought on more fear.

If I were alone, I couldn't hurt anyone, was my thought. This reminds me of the last couple of days that we cared for Hope. Our little hummingbird gained enough strength to fly on her own, and she was getting to the point where she could fly to the top of the cage. We found out that had we left her alone in the cage, she would have become strong enough to fly with force into the top or side of the cage and break one of her wings. Once a hummingbird breaks a wing, they usually die. "It's not good for man to be alone"—or hummingbirds, for that matter either.

Isolation is one of The Prince of Darkness greatest tools. Look at all the homeless people, living their lives in total isolation. From time to time I'll see a homeless person on the street and wonder what is that person's story. Where's their family? What did they do for a living before everything fell apart and brought them to the point to just leave and take to the streets? Isolation is the exact opposite of what God has for us in the way of fellowship and community. Community is where we grow and reach for our potential as human beings.

There's one episode of rage that is very difficult to share, but it illustrates just how deep a dark cloud can envelop a person's life. This happened when I was still pastoring which makes it really embarrassing. I was putting a tile floor down in our bathroom, and it wasn't going well at all. Nan came in, and a typical fight broke out between us. I really have no recollection of what we were arguing about. I somewhat relate to what alcoholics share when they talk about having blackouts. The fight escalated into rage. My remembrance of this episode was that out in our courtyard I was screaming at her, and at one point I grabbed her by the shoulder to try to get her to listen to me.

Later Nan told me that I grabbed her so hard that I bruised her arms. Nan called the police, and they ended up taking me away in handcuffs. I spent the rest of that Saturday in a public jail cell. Later that evening I was released without charges pressed. Nan made a strong point how serious she was about not having rage in our home.

I was angry with her for years for calling the police. This opened me up to a root of bitterness that killed any opportunity to have a healthy relationship. Here's the most humiliating part of this story. The next morning, Sunday morning, I got up and preached as the pastor of the church.

All mental illness carries with it an aspect of deception that cannot be understood until by the grace of God healing comes. Even as I'm sharing this story right now, it sounds so surreal. How could I have gotten up that morning and preached? Boy, when God sheds His light on a situation, you can really see clearly.

It wasn't about the humiliation of what I experienced. I felt in some sick way that Nan betrayed me by calling the police. Still for years after that, rage would still rise up in me. In the back of my mind I would think, *Is this going to be the time that I get hauled off to jail again, but this time not get off so easily and my marriage will be destroyed for good?* I must emphasize once again, I did not have the power to make the choice to stop myself. I just kept spiraling deeper and deeper into a pit of mental illness that started to affect me physically.

> All mental illness carries with it an aspect of deception that cannot be understood until by the grace of God healing comes.

Even knowing what the consequences might be, I felt in some sick way I deserved to be put away. That's what Satan is in the business of doing. Destroying lives and imprisoning people, and making them think that's what they deserve.

This is an illness that is every bit as destructive as alcoholism, drug abuse, or any other form of bondage. The bondage takes on a form of blindness, causing people to grope through the dark fog of deception thinking they can see their way out. This type of illness has to be met by God and the power of His Spirit in His timing. Yes, I did have a choice, but the power of darkness had control of my life, and I continued to make choices to stay in that place. The power of prayer is real, and God does heal. I would find out years later that people had been committed to praying for my mental wellbeing along with the cries of my own heart. God is light and only He can make a pathway out of the darkness with the light of His truth. *Life was in Him, and that life was the light of men. That light shines in the darkness.* (John 1:4-5)

For years I cried out to God to take the depression from me. I supposed I had above-average ability to endure and thought maybe someday God would use this in a positive way. I'll share later how coming to the end of my strength was part of God's plan for me, and frankly anyone else who suffers with rage and depression.

> Life was in Him, and that life was the light of men.
> That light shines in the darkness. (John 1:4-5)

In late August of that same year, Nan and I went to a birthday party of a close friend's son. At that party I thought destiny had finally swung open a door for me to waltz through with the greatest of ease. Through a mutual friend at the party, I ended up working for an estate-planning company as a sales representative. Success came quickly for me.

The first full month with the company I won an award for being top salesman for the month. Three months after that I was offered the corporate sales trainer position. This position only led to further isolation and a fast track to the greatest mistake of my life.

I was commuting eighty-five miles one way to work in the thick of the Los Angeles traffic. Some days it would take me three and half hours to go to or come home from work. That is when I came up with the idea that it might be good for us to move. The commute was really only an excuse to run from my problems: failure with the church planting experience, feelings of *less than* compared to our neighbors, and the pressure of having to face up to my personal failures on a daily basis. All of this was fear-based.

I began to pressure Nan to put the house on the market and move, thinking that moving would be the answer to all my problems. Nan was dead set against the move. After all, this was the house that God provided for her, and her dream was to grow old in that house, with or without me, she said. Frankly, I couldn't blame her for wanting to go on without me in her life. I had given her nothing but heartache with my depression, rage, anger, and self-hatred. Who could live with that and be happy?

Many of the details of how we sold the house are not clear to me. I remember threatening to leave if she didn't sell the house. I said mean and cruel things to Nan to try to make her feel guilty and selfish to want to hold onto a house rather than our marriage. It is only God's grace that she didn't say, "Okay, go ahead, divorce me, and I will keep the house."

Many times since then Nan has told me that she regrets not saying, "I want to keep the house, so go ahead divorce me," and I can't blame her at all. Yes, the biggest mistake of my life was not the sale of our beautiful Spanish hacienda that rested on the top of that hill overlooking some of the most beautiful scenery in all of Southern California. No, the mistake was disrespecting my wife, being abusive to her and succumbing to the fear.

Knowing deep down how that affected my wife and the hurt that I caused her made me go deeper and deeper into the darkness of destruction. I hated myself yet continued to displace my rage on everyone and anyone who came into my path. It would be years before God in His sovereign way would lift the veil of darkness and bring me to my knees before Him, utterly exhausted. Rage does kill. It kills the one who rages and the ones to whom the rage is directed. I couldn't go another day. When it was time, I found myself without any strength to go on.

One of the most difficult yet freeing experiences I've had is to pray with Nan and listen to her cry out to God about every little detail she misses about that house in San Juan Capistrano. It's allowed me to face the pain of failure and destruction in my life and put myself in a position to heal and be used to heal. God and God alone will redeem all of our mistakes. There's nothing that I can do but to trust God to redeem! He really does make all things beautiful in His time. I can say without a doubt *nothing is impossible with God.*

There are many stories I could tell that would illustrate the destruction that rage brings, but my focus is to share the redemptive work that God is doing in me. That's right, *doing,* because that's the operative word. *Doing,* present tense, each and every day for the rest of my life. I don't live in fear of regressing back. I've been set free, delivered and healed. But God continues to change and transform us into His image until we fly free from this world to be with God in eternity. Just like Hope when she was set free from her cage to fly and enjoy the freedom of a world that knows no limits.

> My focus is to share the redemptive work that God is doing in me.

It's my opinion people who suffer with depression and rage must be rescued from these evils. This is an illness that can be healed by the power of our loving God, just like He heals any other disease. Just like when Nan and I rescued Hope, God Almighty came to my rescue. God can and will rescue people from whatever cage they're trapped in. When Hope got hungry, she had a distinct crying little chirp. Nan and I both recognized it when she was hungry, and we heard her cry and fed her. Cry out to God and keep crying until He comes with healing in His wings.

* * *

I love the words to a song called "Healing in Your Wings."

> *There's healing in your wings O Lord*
> *Healing in your wings.*
> *One thing you have spoken*
> *Two things I have heard*
> *That you O God are loving*
> *And my loving God is strong.*
>
> — **Martin Smith**

There is nothing this world can throw our way that can stand up to the strength and love of God.

* * *

Lesson 2:

Set Up for Failure

*Hummingbirds lack a true song. Most of their vocalizations
consist of chirping sounds. They are named for the
humming sound they make through the rapid movement
of their wings when they are in flight.*

MY EARLIEST MEMORIES are about me being
alone somewhere. Loneliness is an early sign of
depression. Or, does depression cause a person to
be lonely? Humans weren't meant to be alone. Prisoners are
put in isolation for punishment. We are made to commune
and be in community. We are designed to interact with others
to learn and teach each other. One of the most powerful gifts
God gives us is the ability to communicate. Communication
is simply to talk and listen to each other and learn from each
other. When we're isolated, personal growth is stunted. God's
plan for our lives cannot come about living a life alone.

I remember when I was four years old being sent to my
grandparents' house because my mother was ill. My grandparents

were going to take care of me. It was supposed to be just for a week, no more than two weeks. It ended up being six weeks. And six weeks to this little four year old seemed like a lifetime. This is where fear first took root in my life.

My grandparents were of Italian descent and predominantly spoke Italian in the home. I didn't speak any Italian other than a few bad words my mother used to call me. Most of the time during the six weeks that I stayed at my grandparents' house, I spent most of my time under an antique bed that was set high enough for a little four-year-old to sit upright underneath it. I would sit under that bed for hours with a little Raggedy Andy doll. The words that describe that little four-year-old sitting under the bed are sadness and fear.

I wonder if I was depressed even then. There's evidence that mental illness can be inherited. My grandfather on my mother's side of the family died in Camarillo State Mental Hospital. What's interesting about that is my mother would always say how much I reminded her of her father. How great is that?

I would sit under that bed and talk to that little doll for hours at a time. I know that my parents and grandparents were trying to do the best they could for me, but I just didn't understand why I couldn't be at home. After all, my older brother and sister got to be at home. Why couldn't I be at home? It had to be my fault that I couldn't be at home. I found out years later that my mother had surgery and complications arose from the surgery. That's why I had to stay with my grandparents longer. "And the truth shall set you free."

This is an example how we get set up at an early age to deal with what life throws at us in unhealthy ways. I learned at the age of four when things get tough, go hide under the bed and isolate. Being lonely is a heck of a lot better than taking the risk to find out the truth. Boy, I bought into that lie real quick and at an early age. I became an expert at running and hiding.

Remember the game hide-and-seek? I thought the goal to that game was to find a spot that no one could find me and just hide out there the entire game. I had my prime spots. One in particular was under this old antique car. The grass underneath this car had grown to the height of the under carriage of the car. So I could crawl under that car and be completely hidden with all the spiders and who knows what else. No one would even have the nerve to look under that car for someone, let alone hide under it. I would lay under there and in some weird way feel *safe from being found out.*

Being found out was not an option for me. I thought that if anyone found out something about me that they would make fun of me, or God forbid not like me. I guess that's because most everyone liked to make fun of me. I never thought that if I revealed a weakness that maybe, just maybe someone might help me to get strength in that area and grow. I developed into a person who would keep secrets so I wouldn't get "found out." Again, this became just another way to isolate and go to that lonely place in life. The nurturing of a small child is so important. To nurture: (to take care of and encourage the growth of).

> I developed into a person who would keep secrets so I wouldn't get "found out."

Another great spot was high up in the biggest tree in the neighborhood. No one ever looked up in that direction so I knew I could climb as high as possible and not be seen or found. You see, I thought the object of the game was to not be found out. I established another destructive behavior—don't be found out or you'll lose.

At the time, I would rather have been lonely under that car or up in that tree than to lose. It was easier to run and hide under a bed, under a car, or high in a tree than to risk being found out. But, those kinds of choices don't work as an adult trying to build lasting relationships. This also taught me to take risks that could be dangerous to myself (like climbing way up in a tree). Why take a risk to reach out to someone when I could risk hurting myself instead? There was some kind of sick thrill with the risk taking. This contributed to the devaluation of self, which translates into low self-esteem. Maybe the risk taking became a way to face the fear that had such a tight grip on my life.

There was one other childhood safe hiding place that I sought out on a regular basis. There was this big metal turtle at the public park in our neighborhood. This turtle resided in the middle of a sand pit where the swings were. I would wait until no one was looking and go crawl under the turtle, and then build up the sand with my hands all around the turtle so I couldn't see out and no one would be able to see in. I would stay under there for long periods of time. That would be my *playtime*. Lonely places are not conducive to building a network of lasting relationships.

Lonely places do allow the work of the darkness to come into your thought life and establish lies that lead to depression. Depression in my life would begin to manifest itself with frustration and anger. The time spent alone and isolated would lead to a sense of worthlessness, which would then lead to frustration and anger inside of me.

Remember the story I shared with you at the beginning of this book about that little hummingbird Hope? If Hope had been left alone in that cage much longer, she would have destroyed herself trying to get out. More than likely, she would have become strong enough to fly into the side or top of the cage and have enough momentum to break a wing and then die. We found out that Hope needed to be put in a cage with other birds to learn how to fly backward, hover, and eventually hunt on her own. Community was the path for that little hummingbird to gain the skills necessary to sustain life.

> The time spent alone and isolated would lead to a
> sense of worthlessness, which would then lead to
> frustration and anger inside of me.

As with that little bird, God calls us to be in relationship with other people and rub up against one other to acquire through relationship the skills necessary to live productive lives for His glory. "As iron sharpens iron, so one man sharpens another" (Proverbs 27:17). Like our little hummingbird, there is growth and freedom in community. I've learned that though isolation and imprisonment may feel familiar, that doesn't make it the healthiest environment to grow and experience freedom.

Most of my childhood was spent playing alone in my room, or playing outside after school alone in my yard. Alone most of the time became an established way of life for a little boy who began to believe that being alone was normal. There were some childhood friendships, the guys in the neighborhood I played ball with, swam with, and went to movies with, but I always found myself hiding under cars, up in trees, or underneath turtles at the first sign of rejection. Alone became very safe, but it sure was lonely.

I will say this about being alone; there were times of peace that looking back I realize that God is with us in our loneliness. He's there looking over us. Just like when Nan and I would go check on Hope in her cage. We would peer down into her cage and make sure she was okay. God does the same thing with us no matter where we are or what we're going through.

I love this psalm. I wish as that four year-old child I could have cried this psalm out to God as a prayer. Try praying this psalm when you are lonely or feeling misunderstood.

Psalm 142: A Cry of Distress

I cry out loudly to God, loudly I plead with God for mercy.

I spill out all my complaints before him,

And spell out my troubles in detail:

As I sink in despair, my spirit ebbing away,

You know how I'm feeling,

Know the danger I'm in,

the traps hidden in my path.

look right, look left—

There's not a soul who cares what happens!

I'm up against it, with no exit—

Bereft, left alone.

I cry out, God, call out:

"You're my last chance, my only hope for life!"

Oh listen, please listen;

I've never been this low.

Rescue me from those who are hunting me down;

I'm no match for them.

Get me out of this dungeon

So I can thank you in public.

Your people will form a circle around me

And you'll bring me showers of blessing!

* * *

Lesson 3:

Sticks and Stones—Ouch

Hummingbird species demonstrate strong territorial behavior; humans might even consider them to be "antisocial."

THE SUNDAY THAT Nan and I gave Hope to the woman who was going to release her, I'd taken Hope outside in our backyard. When I put her cage down on our patio table, it only took a couple of minutes before some hummingbirds were flying around her cage.

We have a tree in our backyard that has big red flowers on the end of its branches that look like bottlebrushes (thus the name bottlebrush tree). Hummingbirds are naturally attracted to these trees. We have hummingbirds in our yard all the time. Most places we've lived, Nan and I have tried to create an environment in our yard to attract birds, especially hummingbirds.

I was excited, thinking that we could possibly let Hope go from our backyard and the other hummingbirds would take her under their wings and teach her the ropes about life outside her cage. The thought that Hope would always come back to our yard as sort of a home base was a wonderful fantasy. I found out later that hummingbirds are extremely territorial, and those other hummingbirds had indeed come to "take care" of Hope. They would have killed her right there on the spot. Hummingbirds don't necessarily receive their own breed. That is a lesson that is sometimes hard to learn.

My junior year of high school I transferred from a large public school to a private school that was much further away from the neighborhood where I grew up. For the first time in my life, I was going to a different school than all my neighborhood buddies. I found myself alone once again. I wasn't well received by my new classmates at the private school and didn't have much in common with the "boys on the block." The fear of rejection overwhelmed me.

It took me half a school year to make friends at my new high school. For some reason it has always been difficult for me to make friends with other men. That rejection added to the depression and rage. Watching those other hummingbirds swarm Hope's cage stirred up some of those memories. I can see now that these things happen in life, and I don't have to be a victim of my past. I can learn from the past and move forward. Good thing I didn't let Hope out of the cage or I would've had another mistake on my list.

Words that are meant with the intention to hurt are like those hummingbirds that came to meet Hope that day. "Sticks and stones will break your bones, but words will never hurt you." What a lie that is. Words are more powerful than any rock or stick I've ever been hit with. The sting and scars that words inflict on a person can last a lifetime and are susceptible to be opened at a moment's notice.

"Sticks and stones will break your bones, but words will never hurt you." What a lie that is. Words are more powerful than any rock or stick I've ever been hit with.

The power of words has the potential to shape who we become or who we may not ever become. Words from our parents can really have a lasting effect on us because they tend to represent and shape our view of God. Our most important relationship is with God, so if we are impacted by the words of man and they influence our view of God, then our ship can sink before it ever sets sail. This is where the importance of be nurtured becomes so important.

I would like to share some words and phrases that have impacted my life in a negative way, because I've found that the force of darkness who is also known as "the accuser of the brethren" or Satan himself doesn't have much of an imagination. I suggest that if any of these phrases hit home with you, then simply take some time to renounce them from your life. You will find a prayer of renouncement at the end of this chapter.

Here we go:

"You're a lazy good for nothing."

"You'll never amount to anything."

"You're such a loser."

"You're so selfish." (Or, self-centered, etc.)

"Children are to be seen and not heard."

"You just need to try harder," or "You're not trying hard enough."

"How stupid are you?" or "You're so stupid".

Here's a good one that an older neighborhood boy said to me when we were playing basketball at the schoolyard with a bunch of friends. I think I was about twelve or thirteen at the time. This was right in the middle of the game when there was a quick break in the action. He looked at me, and right in front of everyone directed these words at me:

"You're the ugliest kid I've ever seen."

Now, that was a fun one I had to deal with for quite a while. The funny thing was looking back, I remember him to have really bad acne, an amazing overbite, and an extra large nose. I would have never thought to share those observations with him in front of his peers in the middle of a basketball game. Life is funny that way.

Although this is not an exhaustive list of negative affirmations/accusations, I think you get the picture. Think about those times when people have done this to you with their words. I would encourage you to release forgiveness and realize that you are not any of those words. It has taken me years to have the freedom to look in the mirror and really appreciate what I see. For years the mirror was my archenemy. When I looked in the mirror I heard those words, *"You're the ugliest kid I've ever seen"*.

What I've found from these *wonderful* childhood experiences is that words spoken over us do not only hurt, but they also create internal patterns that set us up for failure in our relationships with others, our careers, and in our relationship with God Himself.

The most obvious pattern that was established in my life was in the area of anger. I would internalize the hurt and then lash out in some way that I didn't understand at the time. Here's a great example of an experience that haunted me for many years. I don't even remember the words that were directed at me. I just remember vividly my reaction, which caused me to shame myself for most of my adult years.

My brother, who's six years older than me, had a buddy over to the house. As my friend Jimmy and I were coming up the driveway, my brother's buddy made a smart comment toward me that just set me off. So I decided to kick his '56 primer gray Chevy that was his pride and joy. Well that just set him off, and he began to chase me into the house.

The next thing I remember was running into my bedroom and grabbing one of my prized baseball bats and taking a swing for the fences and connecting square with my brother's friend's right knee cap. As he buckled to the floor of my bedroom, I could feel the rage turning into dreaded fear.

I was afraid that when my parents got the bill for a broken kneecap, I would be in trouble for all of my teen years and more. The truth was I punished myself more than any punishment my parents could have ever placed on me. The cycle of fear or anxiety turning into anger and rage then the rage causes depression, which caused the fear to overwhelm me again. This cycle is not easily broken and antidepressants are not the complete answer.

I share this story of the baseball bat to the knee because it's a great example of how displaced anger and hurt can literally destroy relationships, and how the power of words spoken over us can cause us to develop patterns that keep us from moving forward in relationships. Please don't think that I am promoting some sort of sick victimization excuse for this behavior. What I'm trying to communicate is that words can cut deep enough to cause people to view themselves in a way that can bring destruction. There is never any excuse for rage of any form. It must be exposed and must be dealt with so freedom can come. Freedom comes through the truth of how God really sees us so we can come clean and be free from the effects of man's word.

God never condemns a person. God brings life and blessings to us. He would never speak a word to condemn a person's character, appearance, or the core of who he or she is. When God brings freedom, we begin to see ourselves through God's perspective. Our self-esteem begins to grow, and we start to believe that God can do something with our life. Remember we were made in the image of God.

> God never condemns a person. God brings life and blessings to us.

I've learned the practice of not receiving negative affirmations into my life. I mean, never ever receiving negative affirmations. You have to be on the alert at all times. They can come at you at anytime from anyone, many times from the people who love you the most. Now it's important to note that you don't have to be on the defensive. I guess what I'm saying is don't be defensive, or paranoid for that matter. Each morning just ask God to help you to recognize when someone directs a negative statement your way.

You don't have to be religious and say to that person, "I don't receive that in Jesus name." No, you can even in the beginning just whisper under your breath (or just say it silently in your heart) to yourself, "Jesus, I don't receive that and I refuse to let that into my spirit man." Then just move right along. Don't let any time pass to dwell on it. Let the words just fall to the ground and move on. Finally, you might want to add a positive affirmation, something like, "God, I'm your child, and You created me in Your image," or "God, You love me just how I am. There is nothing I have to do or be to earn Your love."

The truth is that words will never hurt me when I allow God to be my advocate and speak truth to me each and every day. Yes, each and every day. Spending time with God each day is a discipline that I'm practicing. I say *practicing* like a doctor practices medicine. They don't have all the answers. They do research, and studies, and sometimes use you and me as "practice patients" to see what works and sometimes what doesn't.

Spending time with God allows me to learn how to take hurts to Him so I don't get in situations and just react. I'm learning the fine art of responding rather than reacting. This takes practice and time. Along the way I've blown it. When I do, I try to be quick to admit that I've blown it. When this practice is working well, it looks something like the following story.

I'm bald. Yes, that's right—no hair on my head. Sometimes friends will make fun of my "beautiful" baldhead. But sometimes someone who may not even know me will make a derogatory comment to put me down to make them look good (go figure—I guess we all do that from time to time when we're feeling insecure).

I can react (and thank God at this point in my healing I don't need to share an ugly story about punching somebody out because they made fun of my bald head) or I can just be quiet and take it to God. This is a simple illustration but sometimes it gets a little more intense than just some comment about a baldhead.

There are times when praying something through is of the utmost importance so a relationship that means something to me doesn't get fractured by some words that were meant to hurt. Forgiveness goes both ways, I'm learning. When I hurt someone with my words, God has from time to time convicted me and I've been moved to go and ask forgiveness.

When someone has offended me with their words I have found that even if they don't ask forgiveness, there is forgiveness waiting for me from my heavenly Father. The love of God our Father removes the sting of words that are meant to hurt.

Here's a sample prayer you can use as a format. I encourage you to make it your own prayer. Be specific and feel free to use your own words to make this prayer real and intimate.

* * *

Dear Jesus, I renounce the power of any word or names spoken over my life in the name of Jesus Christ. In place of the pain that these words have caused me, I receive Your love. And I pray that You would replace them with the words and names that You have for me. Show me the truth that I am your child and you are my Father in tangible ways throughout my day. In the days and weeks to come, I ask You to send people who will speak affirmation over my life, confirming how You view me. I thank You now that the power of these spoken words have been removed from my life and from this day forward I can walk in forgiveness and new life. I receive now the life that Jesus Christ paid for me on the cross. Amen.

* * *

Lesson 4:

"Today"

Obtaining the food needed to live from day to day is a fundamental part of life for birds. Imagine small hummingbirds discovering a large amount of food in one place, such as a feeder. For them a feeder is supernatural. Within a very short time at a feeder, a small, hungry hummingbird can solve its immediate requirements for food.

— **"Give us today our daily bread." Matthew 6:11**

THE OTHER DAY I woke up to just one word. "Today." Yep, that's it, "today." In my mind as I was waking up was the word, "today." It was a bit startling at first. I thought, "What was that, and what about today?" I still don't remember much about that morning and why I heard that single word to start my day, but I've learned a lot recently about "today." That word has stuck with me and I keep learning more lessons about "today."

This chapter is one of those chapters in a book where people say if you're going to read one chapter make sure it's this one. I guess that's what I'm saying (but my hope is you'll read the entire book). Read this with an open mind and ask yourself the question, how significant is today? Or, why is today important?

> This chapter is one of those chapters in a book where people say if you're going to read one chapter make sure it's this one. I guess that's what I'm saying (but my hope is you'll read the entire book).

You've heard the saying, "All we have is today." I believe that more now than ever. I heard a sermon once where the pastor used the analogy of driving a five-speed sports car to illustrate the stages of life. When we're in our twenties, it's like we're in first gear. It seems like we're never going to get going. Then, when we reach our thirties, we move into second gear. We pick up a little speed but we still haven't got it going yet.

In our forties we move into third gear and begin to feel the wind on our face and the potential of the power we have at the wheel. Fifty comes along, and we are just speeding along in fourth gear and everything we pass by is like a blur. Time passes quickly and we think, *did I miss something important along the way? I don't know because I haven't hit sixty yet, but I know fifth gear will allow me to just cruise along and hopefully I'll have learned by then the beauty of enjoying a smooth ride.* I can see myself in a nice comfortable car with the wind blowing across my face just loving the ride. Taking in the beautiful scenery along the way.

So how do we adjust from decade to decade? Many of us baby-boomers suffer from living the dream that never becomes a reality, and we miss out on the "joy of today." We say, *when I get that job then I'll be able to enjoy my life. Or maybe that promotion, or when I get married, or for that matter when I get divorced.* (More people are getting divorced today than are staying married, thinking that's the answer to all their problems how sad is that?)

The grass always looks greener on the other side. Recently I have come to the conclusion that *today* is here and it's here to be lived to its fullest. That's the heart of God when it comes to understanding the potential of today. *Today is a gift from God for all of us to enjoy.* Oh, I may not have all the money I want (or think I need) or the house and car I want, but *today* is really all I have and there is so much life in *today.*

Today is a gift from God for all of us to enjoy.

Each day has enough for us to think about and experience without looking back to the past or looking ahead to the future. Don't get me wrong, I have goals and dreams like everyone else, but I'm learning not to allow the goals or the dreams to interfere with the joy of the moment that's alive in *today.* Slow down, yes, slow down. With all the technology we have at our fingertips, we have the power to move extremely fast through this life.

In reality there's some thirty-somethings who already have the gearshift in fifth gear and have the "pedal to the metal." Slow down! Lesson one to experiencing all that today has to offer is to slow down. What do I mean by that? I'm practicing the fine art of taking time to listen to what people are saying to me. There is so much to be learned from today. Sometimes I spend so much time thinking about yesterday, tomorrow or some unimportant care that I miss out on what people have to offer me. Here's a cliché from my generation that has been so overused that the truth of the statement has lost it power, as you read this cliché slowdown and let the truth of it sink in. Ready,

Stop and smell the roses

Here's a real-life example. Nan was working with a ten-year-old girl who shared with her that she had learned from (get this) a video game how to make the perfect over-easy egg. Now Nan knows that I love my eggs over-easy. Nan asked the girl to share with her the secrets she had learned about cooking eggs over-easy.

This ten-year-old mentor began to unleash the secret to Nan. "After you crack the egg open in the skillet, you drop some water around the edge of the egg and a few drops on the yolk. Cover the skillet with a lid and let it steam." Now get this, I always thought you had to flip the egg, and I would always break the yolk. (I thought over-easy meant flip it over-easy.) Silly me.

Now I make perfect eggs over-easy thanks to Nan's willingness to slow down and learn from a ten-year-old child. Instead of rushing this little over-easy egg princess and her mom out of her office, Nan slowed down and took time out of her busy schedule to learn. That made today valuable for Nan and it sure has made my life less frustrating when I make my eggs over-easy.

Everyone has something to offer you today. Older folks are a treasure of knowledge and have experiences waiting to be drawn upon; they are like a deep well. Your spouse, colleagues, and don't forget the little ones, little children, have the heart of God. So slow down and really listen today. Today can be the day that changes the course of your entire life.

Lesson two regarding today: today may be *the* day. What do I mean by that? I mean, how many times have you heard a person say that their life was going in one direction and all of a sudden *one day* everything just changed? Today may be that day. Each day we live is today. That may sound ridiculously simple, but take some time to let it sink in. Ask God to make today special.

"Help me, God, to make the most of this day. God, help me to go at the pace you want me to go so I don't miss one blessing that you have for me today. I let go of the disappointments of yesterday, and though I look forward to tomorrow, I choose not to worry about tomorrow at the expense of missing what you have for me today."

The day that we found Hope lying in the grass, Nan and I were living life at a leisurely pace and just enjoying a Sunday afternoon. That'll always be a day that I'll look back on and see that God did something very special I'll cherish the rest of my life. Moments like that are what make life exciting to live.

Let me say it this way. Live today like it's the last day of your life. I used to make fun of my wife when she would say, "Lord willing." I would say something like, "Honey, would you like to go away next weekend?" and she would say, "Sure, Lord willing." I've come to appreciate the fact that what she was saying was we don't know what tomorrow will bring. All we have is today.

I've found that when I stay in the moment I experience less anxiety, and way more peace. When my thoughts drift to the failures of yesterday or the unknown of tomorrow I come back to what I know. I know that I have this moment and most of the time it can't get any better than the moment I'm in.

For example, if I'm sitting in traffic, I have the opportunity to thank God and just be with Him for that moment. If I'm doing something fun with Nan or a friend, it doesn't get any better than that. Or, if I'm worshipping with my guitar, or working out, I could go on and on. The truth is, it is in the present moment that I have to enjoy life to its fullest. Do I have all that I want in life at the moment? Absolutely not, but at least I have that moment.

The *present moments* in life get ripped off when we become envious of what others have or jealous, angry, etc. Any negative emotion or feeling that tries to rip off the present moment will just take my joy. I try to always choose to let it go and thank God for what I do have and what He's giving me right then. It's called "just doin' happy" (more on this later).

My biggest enemy is striving. Striving for the things of tomorrow. Striving to try and make yesterday right. I've learned that striving has gotten me nowhere other than lost time and opportunity to enjoy life, to learn from others, and to grow as an individual. Stay in the moment, stay in today, and I guarantee you that life will begin to take a turn for the better.

Finally, today is the time that God has appointed for me to seek Him and His will. If I don't know what He has for me for a given day, I can choose to strive or just waste the day away, or I can make a bold decision to seek God in prayer and simply (and I do mean simply) ask Him, "Show me what you have for me today." God orders and fills my day. Each and every day that I seek Him for what He has is so much more fulfilling, and there's a lot less anxiety.

I know what you're thinking. What if God doesn't say anything? Go forward and He'll lead you. He'll guide you. This is called yielding to Him—are you ready? —*Moment by moment.* Some of my best days are the days when I don't hear anything and just *rest.* It's taken me a lifetime to learn the principles of *rest.*

The Bible speaks of a *Sabbath rest* and I'll address this in detail later, but for now I just want to share some thoughts on this final lesson about living life today. Today is the greatest opportunity I'll have to seek God and to know what He wants for me. Some would call this purpose or call. I like to think of this as walking with God in the garden.

Like when Adam and Eve had the privilege to just be with God. They had no care or worries; all they had was the beauty of being with God in His garden. Just like our little hummingbird, which had no recourse but to just sit and wait for help. She couldn't move, she couldn't help herself out of the predicament that she found herself in, just sitting there stuck in the grass between the leaves. Then Will and Nan showed up. The crazy thing is that the house was already sold and we knew it. We had no reason to be going by that house let alone into the backyard, but God had other plans for little Hope.

Sometimes that's how God works in my life. When I don't know what way to go and I'm just sitting around with little hope, He sends help from the most peculiar places. All God asks of me is to put my trust in Him, enjoy today, rest in today and watch and see what He'll do.

Today

It's a wonderful thought that yesterday is gone because
you and I get to be together again.
Without worry I'm with you. It's taken me so long to
realize the contentment that comes just being with you,
today.
You alone are all I have, and you alone meet my needs,
not yesterday and surely not tomorrow.
The Lord gives you to me, and only you will meet me.
Yes, it's you, today.
Today, I find my place in you when I slow down.
Laughter is in you and blessings as well.
Today, all your benefits are with me.
I will grab hold of you, today.
Good night, today, I look forward to being with you
again tomorrow.
Today

— **Will Cuccia**

Lesson 5:

The Sailboat Race

Hummingbirds use the sun as a "compass." They use the sun's position in the sky—and where it is at different times of day—to stay on course.

THIS PAST SUMMER, Nan and I had the privilege of participating in a sailboat race. Nan has a client who has a sailboat and loves to sail. His wife doesn't enjoy sailing because she gets seasick quite easily. So Bill (the sailor) is always looking for someone with whom to sail. Nan and I have always wanted to learn how to sail, so it seemed only natural for us to take Bill up on his offer to go sailing. He asked if we wanted to go with him on a local Friday evening race in the harbor. Well, we jumped at the opportunity.

I'm pretty competitive by nature, I played every sport as a kid, and the first twelve years of my professional adult life (after the military) I taught high school math and coached football, basketball, baseball and track. When I say I hated losing, I mean I h-a-t-e-d losing. I always coached to *not lose*. I know that is the worst kind of motivation. I didn't understand the joy of the pursuit and being satisfied with doing your best. I hated losing!

Nan and I had the wonderful experience of falling into dead last position in our first sailboat race. Poor Bill, he was trying so hard to catch a good wind and tack at the right times, and it just seemed to get worse with every strategic move that he would attempt. It didn't help that Bill had Nan and me as his crew. What was intriguing about this sailing experience was that Bill had a GPS navigation system on board that would give us the direction we were headed and how many degrees our course was off the buoy that we had to race around. This GPS unit also told us how far away the buoy was in time.

We would go from being 30 minutes away to 20 and back to 29 or 30 minutes again. Now understand I'm not much of a sailor. As a matter of fact, this was my third sailing experience of my life. But I did understand that if we were only 15 minutes from the buoy and all of a sudden we were now 20 minutes away, we had somehow gotten off course and were now farther away.

Poor Bill, just after we finally got around the buoy and were on our way home and realized that we were dead last, he piped out, "Well, I guess this is just not our day to catch a good wind." Nan's response was, "But it sure is peaceful out here." Bill with a sigh said, "Yeah, real peaceful." I just busted up laughing; it was so funny to see the different perspectives. The truth is, it was peaceful. I had lost sight of winning the race, and I was just enjoying being out on the open water. It didn't matter to me that there wasn't any wind and we were not winning the race. I knew we were going to finish, and that's all that mattered. It was fun to be out on the open water in a sailboat.

The GPS system gave me confidence that at some point the wind would pick up and we would be able to sail in. The GPS system told us how many knots we were traveling, where we were and where we needed to be to stay on course. What else did I need to give me confidence that everything was going to turn out okay? I have access to a GPS system in my own life. I call it "God's Prayer System." I get up every day and ask God to guide me. I ask Him to give me direction. I ask Him to keep me on course. I think you get it. When I let go of trying to win and trust that God is in control of my life (and that includes how fast I go), life is much more peaceful and enjoyable. The key is keeping my eye on the GPS system and not on my circumstances.

What was really funny about that sailboat race was that Bill decided after his valiant effort to catch some wind he would make up for lost time by taking the sails down and just motoring in. That allowed us to get in before any of the other racers and meet Bill's wife for a lovely dinner at the yacht club. Yes, we didn't win the race, but we sure did enjoy a peaceful afternoon out on the open water and still got in ahead of everyone else.

I'm learning that I don't always have to win, but I can slow down and trust God and His plans for my life and still reap incredible benefits here on earth. God can choose to turn on the motor at anytime and get me where He wants me to be. When I let God be the captain of my ship, life is easier and I'm less frustrated with everyone else getting ahead. I can take my eyes off the race and just look to the GPS system and enjoy where I'm at that moment and enjoy the experience. The best part of that afternoon was being out on a sailboat with Nan, and getting to make a new friend in Bill. Life really is about the people and not about winning.

Lesson 6:

Our Cat Boaz

*I had to devote one chapter to my beloved cat Boaz, so
we'll take a break from Hope. This is for all you cat lovers.
I'm sure you'll relate.*

WE HAVE A cat name Boaz. Yes, I named him Boaz after the character in the Bible, Boaz. Boaz, the one in the Bible, is an Old Testament character that is an example of Jesus Christ. Boaz was a kinsmen redeemer (which means he was the nearest relative so he had first choice to redeem Ruth if he wanted), and he redeemed Ruth (in the Bible) to be his wife. That's what Jesus did for us. Jesus is our *Kinsmen Redeemer.* Jesus gave His life for us so we can have life.

Anyway, that's why I named my cat Boaz. I wanted to give him a regal name. Nan wanted to name him Confetti. It doesn't really matter because Nan calls the cat Bobo most of the time and I call him Bodee. Neither name is very regal, but I can tell you that our little cat, no matter what we call him, lives a very regal life. Have you ever thought about the life of a cat?

Our little Boaz gets fed at least three times a day. He sleeps most of the day (in his favorite sun spots around our house), and he wakes us up at six a.m. every morning. I don't know how he knows it's six a.m. but when I get to heaven I'm going to ask God how that little creature was able to keep such accurate time without knowing how to read a clock.

Boaz wakes us up each morning (I'm going to say it once more for effect) at six a.m. by scratching on our door. He starts out real soft. The sound is actually a little pleasant to wake up to. If we don't respond, he starts scratching louder and louder and louder. If we don't respond to that, he begins to throw his body against the door. It sounds like a grown person pounding on the door, and I do mean an adult pounding on the door. It sounds like a 250-pound linebacker pounding his way through the line of scrimmage to get to the quarterback.

I think you get the picture. When the pounding gets that loud, Nan or I respond and give him the attention needed. I must confess ninety percent of the time it is Nan who responds for two very good reasons. First, she has much more compassion for that little creature then I do, and second, at the point when the pounding is the loudest I remind myself; "It's really her cat anyway, and Boaz really loves her more than me." That justifies me staying in bed quite well. Boaz's pounding on the door usually means it's time for breakfast and he's ready to eat. Once Boaz is fed; he's quite pleasant again and we can go back to sleep. I mean, Nan comes back to bed and joins me again as I'm already asleep.

Our relationship with God is very similar in many ways. The Bible tells us that when we are in need we're told to ask, seek, and knock. We have a heavenly Father who (though He never sleeps) is waiting for us to come to Him with our needs. I think more important than understanding that God is waiting, it is important to understand that my cat waits for us to open that door each morning. He knows which door to go to because he trusts that we're there and will open the door.

Nan and I like to travel. We love to go and experience the world. We have a real wanderlust. Many times when we have been away, I wonder what Boaz does in the morning. I wonder if he still shows up at our door or if he knows we're not there. Maybe he knows we're not there because he can't smell us, who knows? I certainly don't because I'm not there.

And that's my point. We're not there, but God who is faithful is always there. He never fails us. He never goes on vacation. He is always waiting at the door when we knock. That's where I put my hope. I think of Hope, our hummingbird. At just the right time, the lady that Nan and I left Hope with will choose to open up her cage and let her fly free. That lady's an expert and knows when's the best time to let Hope fly free.

I question God all the time about His timing in answering my prayers. It seems like I'm knocking on the right door and I know He's in there, but God just doesn't come to the door to feed me. I have to trust that God is a good Father and He knows what time it is and what's best. I have to make a choice to trust God will open the door. I don't have to sit at the door and beg or throw my body against the door to get His attention. I can just wait at the door in faith knowing that He will answer in the best timing for my benefit.

> I have to trust that God is a good Father and He knows what time it is and what's best.

Just one last thought about my cat, Boaz. There are times that he'll be sitting at the door of our bedroom just waiting in the hall for us to open the door. This morning was one of those times. When I opened the door, there was Boaz looking up at me, sitting so patiently just waiting. I looked down at that precious little creature and said, "Oh Bodee, do you want to come into Mommy and Daddy's room?" He looked up at me and without any hesitation just strolled right past me into the bedroom where he belongs. You see, Boaz is confident that he has access into our room and he boldly walks through the door. I think that God is pleased when we respond in confidence and boldly trust Him for where He has called us to go.

Lesson 7:

The Eyes of Hope

Hummingbird eyes are large and immobile, with both monocular and binocular vision. Both eyes will typically outweigh the brain.

I WON'T EVER FORGET the day we found Hope in that backyard and saw her little eyes peering up at us through the grass and leaves where she had somehow landed. Those eyes, piercing and dark ("Your eye is the lamp of your body," Luke 11:34), were crying out for help. Her eyes looked lost and helpless. Have you ever seen anyone with those kinds of eyes? I think I do every day. There are people crying out for help with their eyes. Strangers in the streets, family members in our homes, co-workers in our places of employment—they are everywhere.

I used to see them in that dreaded mirror in my bathroom when I looked at myself real close. I didn't know that's what I was looking at; I thought I was looking at ugly, or stupid. Those were the old words that people used to try and put me down with, whatever their reason. When I think back on the moment when I first looked into Hope's eyes, I saw the same thing in my own eyes. I remembered what it was like to look at myself in the mirror after I had raged at Nan, at someone at work, or in my neighborhood. I felt once again hopelessly depressed that I would never be able to overcome my faults on my own. The shame was suffocating. The fear of the rage reoccurring was overpowering.

There's no way that Hope could have found her way back to the nest and be back in a safe place of nurturing. Her eyes spoke loud and clear. Heck, Nan and I couldn't even find her nest. Nan and I have talked about what if we had found Hope's nest and put her back. Would she have been safe? Maybe we were supposed to find her. Maybe her destiny at that moment was to be found and transported to a place to be cared for and nurtured and then move on to be free to live the life for which she was destined.

It's so hard to try and figure out why things happen the way they do in our lives. Just a couple of nights ago I couldn't sleep, and I was struggling with a question for which I didn't have an answer. "God, why did it take so long for me to get deliverance and healing?" This question came from way down deep inside of me just after midnight. That question provoked another question, *why didn't this come earlier in my life so I wouldn't have to suffer through the heartache of a wounded marriage and put my wife in such a vulnerable place?* I thought, *why couldn't God have just kept us from the pain that all this living hell had caused?*

Why couldn't I've just made the right choices, choices not to rage, not to allow myself to fall into the pit of depression so many times? Well, I don't have the answers, but I know one thing. I'm a changed man today.

Remember how important it is to stay in today, right? There are lessons that can be learned when we take the time to allow ourselves the freedom to just rest and wait. Sometimes I strive so hard to get the answers that I send myself into a place that is not productive. Sometimes I have to sit there and wait for someone to come and help me get to where I need to be. I can see it in my eyes.

Have you ever been someplace like a shopping mall or a public park and got separated from the person you were with? One Saturday Nan and I went to this little mall to see some pottery that she wanted to show me. At one point I drifted off to look at one shop and Nan went the other way. I spent a good bit of time walking around in circles looking to catch up with Nan or run into her. Finally, I decided to just stay put and let her come around to where I was.

That was the place Hope was that day when we found her, just hopelessly waiting. But was it hopeless? No, there was someone leading us to find her. Yes, God is at work even when we feel we are in situations that look hopeless to us. God is preparing, God is sending help, and He's positioning people to be in the right place at the right time for you. He is the God of Hope.

Maybe I misread that look in Hope's eyes. Could it be trust or maybe contentment? Could it be that she was waiting in faith, with the knowledge that help would come? She may not have known when the help was coming, but she had the confidence in her Maker that help would come. Could she have been on her way into another state of torpor (slowing down her heart rate) and resting in the fact that help was on its way?

> She may not have known when the help was coming, but she had the confidence in her Maker that help would come.

I would like to think that what I saw in her eyes wasn't despair, or concern. No, what I saw was a quiet confidence that even though she didn't have all the answers, she found trust in something bigger than her circumstances. She knew deep down in her "knower" that help was imminent. She had resolved that someone bigger than her ability to save herself was in complete control.

The answers to the questions become unimportant if I keep my mind fixed on these truths. God is in control, and no situation is too hopeless for God. I don't know what you may be going through, but I know as a result of my life that God does deliver, heal, and ultimately restore people and relationships, and many times to a state better than the original. Hope is found in God alone.

I just didn't read this stuff in a book. I got the privilege to live through it. I can look in the mirror now and see a beautiful new creation that my Creator made. I am not ugly or stupid. I look in the mirror and see eyes of hope. God rescued me. I didn't find my way through a twelve-step program or church. (These are great resources, and I know people find healing from these places every day.) God is making something beautiful out of my life and I can see hope in my eyes for the first time in quite a while. When I look in the mirror I see light in my eyes again, I can see the life coming back and that's a beautiful reality.

For some reason God looked down at me and saw my eyes of desperation peering up at Him, and He picked me up and touched my life.

If God can do that for me, He can do that for you as well. Somehow I found the strength one morning to cry out for help, and God said it was time. Does it really matter today in the midst of my joy for life that He didn't do it sooner?

Lesson 8:

Hope Falling

Fledglings normally will jump or fall out of the nest.
This is their "flight training" stage.

TODAY IS ANOTHER Sunday, and I'm at church listening to our pastor teach a sermon on purity in relationships. As I sit here, I wonder what Hope felt when she was falling from her nest to the ground. Or did the mama bird accidentally knock her out of the nest or drop her and wasn't able to find her or even know she was missing?

I think about how many times in life I've fallen spiritually, emotionally and even a few times literally fallen. One time in particular, I was washing some windows on a two-story house on Balboa Island. It was early in the morning and the wood shake shingles on the roof were not only wet but were covered in moss.

After I had finished the windows I realized it was time to navigate my way down the roof to the ladder so I could climb down. I was wearing some tennis shoes with smooth bottoms (not a particularly smooth move on my part). I realized I couldn't get down without sliding, so I decided to bend my knees so my bottom was resting on my heels, thinking I could slide down the roof to the latter and then just grab onto the ladder.

As I began my descent, my speed began to increase. By the time I reached out for the ladder, my momentum caused the ladder to go sideways. At that point I think I felt a little bit of what Hope may have felt as she was falling. It's called *out of control*. I hit the concrete driveway with my hip and elbow first. As I lay on the pavement I tried to figure out what in the heck had gone wrong. My plan had seemed like a good one. My thoughts went from *I wonder if anything is broken* to *I wish my wife were here right now to help me.* No one was actually around, and I wasn't sure if it was wise for me to move. After lying there a few minutes I decided to try and get up on my own. I was able to gather myself but I think I was in some level of shock.

> At that point I think I felt a little bit of what Hope may have felt as she was falling. It's called *out of control*.

When I arrived at my next client's home I knew something was wrong based on her response when she opened the door. Before I could say a word she looked at me and said what happened to you. She said something like, "You look like you just saw a ghost." After I explained what happened, she urged me to get to a doctor or go straight to the hospital. She offered to call my wife so she could come and pick me up (this was before the days of cell phones). Frankly, I was glad that she offered to call and get me some help.

I'm sure that Hope was also in shock when we found her. Shock seems to go along with any type of a fall. I tend to always think about how in the world did I end up there? How did this happen to me? I was going in one direction and all of a sudden I found myself falling. How can I stop myself from falling? I wondered how Hope fell? Did she go end over end? Did she try to flap her wings on the way down to attempt to save her? Or did she just do one of those feet-first straight drops and plummet to the ground?

What's amazing to me is that Hope landed without injury. That day I fell off the roof; the only injury I sustained was a bruised elbow (that's elbow not ego). It is amazing that sometimes people are able to avoid serious injury in the midst of an accident. I have heard stories of people who have fallen much shorter distances than I fell that day and either died or are paralyzed. I know this because the doctor that I went to that day made it very clear how fortunate I was to have escaped serious injury let alone be alive.

I think *it's truly a miracle that Hope made it through her fall alive*. Given her size (about two inches tall) and the distance of her fall (at least eight to ten feet), it's truly amazing. She couldn't even fly when Nan and I first found her, so flying wasn't an option to break her fall.

That day in church, I didn't get much out of my pastor's message but I did learn a valuable lesson once again. That God is sovereign and He's in control of our destiny. Time is in His hand, and if I trust Him He will always be there to meet me. Even when I fall, He will be there to catch me and get me to the next stage in my life.

"The God of old is [your] dwelling place, and *underneath* are the *everlasting arms*. He drives out the enemy before you, and commands, Destroy!" (Deuteronomy 33:27). God alone is the one who keeps us from harm's way. He is our protector. Just like God protected Hope that day when she fell to the ground, He's protecting me through each and every move that I make. I'm sure that when I fell that day God had my guardian angel right there to cushion my fall. I wonder if hummingbirds have guardian angels?

After the fall, I wondered what was going on in that little hummingbird's head. *What just happened to me, and when is my mama going to come and swoop me up and place me back in my nest? Is she going to reprimand me for being too close to the edge of the nest?* I raise these questions because with each fall that comes in life, there are emotional and spiritual ramifications that come into play that can have lasting effects on who we are and how we respond in relationships. I wonder if *Hope* had the thought, *Boy, I'm never going to try that again.* Falls tend to make me think that way. They make me gun shy. They take some of that gunslinger mentally out of me.

I tend to think about approaching life more safely in the future. I'm not so sure if that is the lesson that God wants me to learn when I fall. Maybe, just maybe, He wants me to get right back up on that roof and wash some more windows, knowing that valuable lessons come with experience that will help me the next time I'm in that situation. I knew one thing, if I ever went up on that roof again it would be in different shoes, at a different time of the day, and I would surely have a better exit plan in place to get down from the roof. Sometimes experience brings wisdom with it.

Life is full of falls. There are going to be times when I tumble and get scrapes, but that can't keep me from trying again. After all, what if God allowed Hope to fall just so Nan and I would find her and have the experience to learn all these lessons? It's a win-win. I get to learn valuable lessons that have really caused me to think about how much God does love, care, and wants me to grow up and accomplish something, and Hope was taken care of.

There was a commercial on television that ran last year in which this famous basketball player is shown at different stages in his career, high school, college, and then at the professional level. At each level, the commercial shows him falling or getting knocked down. At the end of the commercial, it says, "fall down seven times, get up eight." When we stop falling down is when we stop learning, risking, trying new things. I don't ever want to stop learning, growing, or living. Falling is just part of life. How we respond is what matters.

I had a vision of myself once in diapers at the age of around two years old. In the vision I was trying to run, not walk. I took a few steps and did a face plant. I got up, just like a little two year old would, and as I turned back in the direction that I tried to run from, Jesus was sitting there with His arms open to me with a smile on His face. It was the kind of smile that a father has when one of his kids has just tried something and he's proud that his child made the attempt. I ran into His arms, and He scooped me up and held me. It felt so good to feel His arms around me. Just because we take a leap of faith and it doesn't turn out the way we thought doesn't mean that God abandoned us. There are lessons to be learned even in the fall. If we fall it doesn't mean we'll never fly again. The experience of falling sometimes allows us to have the ability to fly higher the next time.

Lesson 9:

Good Intentions

I found a baby hummingbird. Now what?

The first thing you should do is nothing! Look around: is the bird's mother waiting for you to leave so she can feed it? (Only the mother participates in the nesting duties.) Occasionally, hummer nestlings fall over the side, but, like other birds, the parent rarely abandons them.

AFTER THE THIRD day of taking care of Hope we began to realize that her fuzzy little under feathers (the ones under her neck and down her belly) were beginning to look red in color. It was the same red color that was in the sugar water that we were feeding her. Our carpet cleaner came by to clean our carpets, and it just so happened that his mother raises birds. Well, our carpet cleaner shared with us that we needed to put some water in a bowl so Hope could bathe. He also let us know that it wasn't good for Hope to have that sticky sugar water on her feathers.

Well, that's all I needed to hear, I immediately put some water in a bowl and placed it in Hope's cage. Our carpet cleaner said to be sure to not put too much water in the bowl because a bird that small could drown in the water if she were to fall in. I was careful to not put too much water in so this would not happen. See I would have put a whole bunch of water in a bowl so Hope could take a nice big bath. The kind of bath I like to take. Good intentions, right?

Later that evening guess what happened? That's right. Hope fell in the water and was stuck and couldn't get out of the water. Nan found her first, and it freaked her out. She was able to get Hope out of the water and save her from potential calamity. The intentions were well meaning, but the results were not. Had we gone out to dinner or had not checked on her for a certain length of time that could have meant Hope's demise.

Good intentions don't always work out. Good intentions are just what they are. Good intentions don't always get good results. Hope and the water bowl could have ended with a terrible result. The motive was definitely pure on our part to give Hope the ability to bathe. I've thought about "good intentions" a lot lately. Here are some of the lessons I've learned from Hope and the water bowl.

How many times have I heard these words, "I had good intentions," or "My intentions were good. I didn't mean to hurt you." I wonder if I were to take the time and think about all the possibilities of what could happen with my "good intentions," would I have still said, "I had good intentions"? Then I thought, *there's no way I can know all the possibilities.* The truth is that as good as my intentions may be, I may still put someone I love or myself in danger.

The conclusion I came to is that in life, good intentions don't get me much, but I can't stop trying to do what I think is good. That means a lot to me at this point in my life. But here is where the freedom comes. When I blow it, I can ask for forgiveness. I can say, "What I did or said was wrong. Will you forgive me?" That is always where the freedom and the healing begin and end. Rather then trying to defend my actions with the "good intentions" plea I can just say, *I blew it will you forgive me?*

> The conclusion I came to is that in life, good intentions don't get me much, but I can't stop trying to do what I think is good.

Even as I wrote this, I remembered that when Nan and I were getting Hope out of the water bowl, I found myself saying, "Oh little bird, I'm sorry." I wonder if I really meant, "My intentions were good." There was really nothing I could've done to make it absolutely safe for Hope so she wouldn't fall in. Life has risks, and we all mean well most of the time. When we blow it, the best way to remedy any situation is to ask forgiveness. The good news, there's a happy ending to this lesson. Hope was able to clean herself and not get sick from having her feathers all sticky with sugar water.

I can remember years would go by and I wouldn't ask forgiveness. I thought that the fact that my intentions were good was all that was necessary. It didn't matter that my good intentions were causing people to drown, especially my wife. All that mattered was that my intentions were good, or so I rationalized year after year as I left destruction along my path.

No, relationships do not grow through good intentions. Relationships are nurtured through forgiveness and the healing that forgiveness brings. Who cared what my intentions were anyway? What matters now is when I do blow it (no matter what my intentions), I simply try asking forgiveness and admitting I was wrong. I learned years ago from a pastor friend that to say, "I'm sorry" is not good enough. He said if you say I'm sorry to your wife she should respond with *sorry for what? The proper way to ask forgiveness is to admit what you did wrong and ask for forgiveness.* Something like this, *what I said to you was wrong will you please forgive me?* Try it. It's amazing how people will respond to a sincere request for forgiveness. Forgiveness builds relationships.

> No, relationships do not grow through good intentions. Relationships are nurtured through forgiveness and the healing that forgiveness brings.

A few days before my final meltdown, I was driving home from work. It was another late evening. I was tired and I just wanted to get in my house and crash from another day of work. As I drove down my street, there were a bunch of neighbors in front of my garage with their dogs. I thought, "I don't need this," so I just kept driving up to my garage. I slowed down, but I wanted to make the point that I was in control and I wasn't going to take any grief. One of our young neighbors thought he would be the hero and started to pop off at me. I said some things to him (that I'm not proud of), and it escalated from there. Once again I had shamed my wife and myself.

A couple of weeks after the confrontation with the neighbors and the dogs, I was coming home in the afternoon and was going into my front door when I heard that young neighbor in a mocking tone yell out to me, "Hey, Pastor, how's it going?" I didn't have the strength to even try to respond. I just looked at him and turned and went into my house.

A few months passed, and I saw that same neighbor. I walked up to him and asked his forgiveness. I said, "Listen, that day that I popped off to you I was wrong for acting that way. I could make all kinds of excuses for my behavior and what I was going through at the time, but it doesn't matter. What I did was wrong, so please forgive me." He accepted my apology and then tried to justify his behavior, but I didn't care. I received the freedom that forgiveness offers. Now that same neighbor reaches out to me every time he sees me with friendship.

Asking forgiveness set me free. It allowed me the freedom to move on without the shame of my behavior. That's what forgiveness can do if we truly forgive ourselves when we blow it. We're going to blow it—that's a given. When we blow it, the quicker we ask forgiveness and forgive ourselves the more freedom we can experience in life. I had a taste that day of what Hope must've felt when she flew from her cage for the first time.

Every time we take the risk to ask forgiveness and receive forgiveness it allows us to grow stronger so we can fly farther.

Lesson 10:

Expectations

A hummingbird's wing muscles make up about 25% of their overall weight as compared to 5% pectoral muscle weight in human beings.

I WONDER WHAT IT must be like for *Hope* in the big wide world without the protection of her cage. How does she cope from day to day? A big part of her existence is to hunt for food. But how would she cope in the wild without Nan and me to look after her? Would she be okay out there? What if some predator came and tried to harm her? This is the type of stuff I used to worry about for my own life. At least I could take care of myself, or so I thought. Could Hope survive out there? Or was she afraid?

These are the same questions that I find myself asking about my own personal flight into the great big world we call life. For so many years I lived as a victim of depression and rage. They were crutches for me walk through life. Now they're not available. Will I ever walk with a natural gait? I shared earlier how I would sabotage situations so I wouldn't have to deal with the pain of getting hurt by someone's cruel words.

I would sting first before someone could sting me. That's not an effective way to build relationships or a successful life. It's almost like I have to learn how to live life all over again. I don't have the same anxious feelings that would overwhelm me in certain situations. The absence of anxiety causes me to wonder if this is normal. Is this how most people feel all the time? I lived life in this constant fear of being found out. I'd become anxious about the simplest interactions, constantly feeling like a child in the midst of a world of adults.

Now I find myself calm in most situations, not worried about what others might think about me. My confidence isn't in what others think about me. When I was ten years old, an older boy in the neighborhood molested me over a three-year period. I remember he would tell me not to tell anyone because I would get in a lot of trouble if anyone found out, *especially my parents.* I would get really sick to my stomach when he would come to our house to see if I could play. I wonder if this was the source of anxiety gripping my life? Being found out began to hold a lot of power. This power would paralyze me. I didn't know what was the right thing to do. I would get angry with myself for not being able to stand up to this kid. I knew in my heart I had to tell someone, but I was so full of the fear of being found out. I felt so dirty but I didn't know how to get clean. So I fell into the pattern of isolation. At school I would slip back into the pattern of isolation. I began to act out and get in trouble in school. Maybe I thought someone would realize that I was crying out for help. Many days I just spent daydreaming through my classes trying to escape the painful reality of my life.

> I remember he would tell me not to tell anyone because I would get in a lot of trouble if anyone found out, *especially my parents.*

When I got home from school I would go out in our backyard and just play baseball by myself. I felt safe in the backyard. I knew if the kid who was molesting me came to the front door, no one would answer because I was home alone. I created an imaginary world of safety for myself from 3:00 in the afternoon until 5:00 when my sister or one of my parents came home. I was part of the original latchkey generation.

I began to figure out ways to keep myself safe, but it still didn't make me feel good about who I was. Looking back I realize that patterns were being established to bring on the deadly cycle that comes with depression and rage. It starts with anxiety then anxiety becomes fear. At some point the fear or flight instinct kicks in. Either way leads to anger and anger becomes rage.

The molestation caused me to be alone too much during a critical time of my adolescence years. As a result of all those lonely hours the destructive cycle of depression and rage grew deep roots. I transitioned into my teenage years a cloudy mental mess of confusion. I didn't have a clue of who I was. I knew I was angry; I just didn't know why. Once I received healing and deliverance, my head felt clear for the first time in my life, and I found there was an absence of anxiety. For the first week my head felt empty, without thoughts. It actually felt good. I felt free. Being empty headed isn't all that bad.

> The molestation caused me to be alone too much during a critical time of my adolescence years. As a result of all those lonely hours the destructive cycle of depression and rage grew deep roots.

I think about the freedom that Hope has now; she can fly anywhere she wants. Yes, there's danger out there of which she has to be aware, but it's got to be so much better than life in a cage. Hope was created to fly free and not be cooped up in some cage. Her body was built to fly, and hover, and hunt for food. A hummingbird's wing muscles make up about 25% of their overall weight as compared to 5% pectoral muscle weight in human beings.

Like Hope, I was made for a unique purpose as well. Everyone is uniquely designed for a specific purpose. Birds are made to fly. So what was I made for? What was I made to do? This became my quest as I prepared myself to leave my cage for good. There's a transition period where Hope is put in a bigger cage, more like an aviary, but what makes this aviary different than the cage we put Hope in is that this cage doesn't have a roof. Hope can come and go until she's ready to "fly the coop for good." This is another part of her preparation to be ready to take on the "brave new world." This is called a soft release.

Sometimes I feel I'm in that soft release stage. God lets me venture out, and when I fall on my face He allows me to fly back to that place of safety. Even though God knows that it's not best for me to go back to the aviary, He knows I need it. A "soft release" in Hope's case is a gradual return to the wild whereby an animal receives support, shelter and food until it's entirely able to fend for itself. Often, a soft release takes place from a release cage or an aviary on-site.

After Hope has spent time in the outdoors enclosure, she becomes familiar with the sights, sounds, smells, etc., of the area, and is aware of the activity of other wildlife. She can return to the enclosure for food or shelter when necessary. Food and water is left outside the enclosure as well.

In a spiritual sense, I think of the local church as our soft release aviary. I was stunted in my growth because I spent too long in a cage that held me captive. I didn't transition to the "soft release aviary" (church or community). The deception of my mental illness for years said, "Isolate, you don't need anyone else." That's a big lie people buy into. The prince of darkness doesn't want us to be in community where we can grow and learn about how to live life in "the wild."

That's the beauty of a place like Starbucks or any meeting place where people come together. Community happens in those places and that is a powerful place for growth to occur.

I have listed below the health requirements for birds that are ready to move into a soft release environment. I found this quite interesting.

* * *

- The bird should be free of disease and/or parasites.
- Its weight should be the same as the average for wild of its own species of the same age.
- If the bird had an injury, it should be fully healed. If the bird has a permanent handicap (e.g., poor sight in one eye, poor grip in one foot), it must demonstrate that it can compensate. It's crucial to know the bird's method of foraging. A bird of prey must have the ability to grasp and kill prey with its feet. A bird of prey or an aerial insectivore must have 100% normal flight if it is to catch adequate food. A bird must have a strong, normal bill.
- A bird must be able to perch. A bird with a splayed leg cannot keep the limb warm in inclement weather and may encounter problems with frostbite. A water bird that needs a long "runway" for take-off (e.g., loon) must have two healthy legs (and feet).

The bird must sustain flight without tiring, panting, trembling, etc. If the bird is an aerial insectivore, it must demonstrate the ability to catch prey in flight. If the bird is a leaf-gleaning insectivore or a hawking insectivore (flies from a branch to catch prey), it must demonstrate the ability to catch insects.

* * *

What does this all mean? A whole lot of care and concern goes into determining when little Hope will be ready to move into the wild and fend for herself. She has to be healthy and strong. She has to be able to endure the elements on her own. She must develop the skills, talents and abilities to function in the wild on her own. Do you get it? Everyone benefits from good old-fashioned nurturing. The popular word today is coaching or professional mentors.

It's a mentoring process if you will. That's the purpose of community today. In community we get mentored, we receive coaching from people who care about us, right? People who can function in the world and make an impact. No longer crippled by some set of religious rules or some humanistic philosophy, but become people who can go out and love other people. This is what's called making disciples.

This is a detailed analogy of what it means when the Bible describes "making disciples" or in modern day language, to be mentored. Or maybe the best way to describe this is with the word I talked about earlier, to nurture (to take care of and encourage the growth of). Nurturing builds trust—trust in the person who is coaching you and trust in the abilities you develop in the process of being nurtured.

Healing is an ongoing process. I experience the greatest amount of slippage when I take my eyes off the prize and think about what's in it for me. The Apostle Paul describes the prize this way: "I pursue as my goal the prize promised by God's heavenly call in Christ Jesus" (Philippians 3:14). Paul is talking about knowing Christ; it's about knowing Christ more and more each day that we are here on earth.

I tend to slip into the "what about me?" syndrome. *What am I going to be? What was I made for? Have you forgotten me, God?* See, the focus is all about me. I've got to keep my eye on the goal and everything else will be taken care of. And the Church and community of believers is there to train, nurture and hold each other accountable when we do stumble. The call of the Church should be, "No more victims." When I slip into the victim mentality, Nan is quick to call me to account. I hate it, but she's right and I love her for it. My prayer, "God let the Church build up and encourage the growth of people, help the Church to nurture people along, and everyone said a big healthy amen."

When I was in my descent and was falling fast, my heart was stirred to read Matthew, chapter six. This is a well-known passage of scripture, and I would like to share in the next lesson what I learned from this passage through the "eyes of Hope" (that precious little hummingbird—I owe you a lot little fellow).

> "God let the Church build up and encourage the growth of people, help the Church to nurture people along, and everyone said a big healthy amen."

Lesson 11:

Send Your Light

"If you decide for God, living a life of God-worship, it follows that you don't fuss about what's on the table at mealtimes or whether the clothes in your closet are in fashion. There is far more to your life than the food you put in your stomach, more to your outer appearance than the clothes you hang on your body. Look at the birds, free and unfettered, not tied down to a job description, careless in the care of God. And you count far more to him than birds."
— Matthew 6: 25, 26 (The Message)

HUMMINGBIRDS ARE THE smallest birds in the world. For their size, they have the largest heart and brain of all animals. They have no sense of smell, and their wings beat around sixty times per second. Hummingbirds visit 2,000 to 5,000 flowers a day. They can consume twice their weight daily. Their color is produced by refraction of light, not by pigment. Their average speed is forty-five miles per hour.

Their tongues are twice the length of their bills. In addition to nectar, hummingbirds eat insects for protein. Hummingbirds can't walk, only perch. Hummingbirds fly only 20% of the time.

Okay, so how much more does God care for us? If God is that detailed about the smallest bird in creation, how much more does He care for you and me?

That day I saw Hope on the ground, I thought, *what a little creature that is.* The next thing I knew, Nan (with her compassion for animals) had me figuring out a way to take her home. It didn't take long to figure out that if God cared that much about a little creature to let us find her and bring her home, how much more does He care for us human types?

Jesus said it this way, as he was teaching his disciples, "If God gives such attention to the appearance of wildflowers—most of which are never even seen—don't you think he'll attend to you, take pride in you, do his best for you?" (Matthew 6:30, The Message). Since I've been healed, I've learned the importance of trusting God, putting my faith in Him, and believing each day that He will care for me.

Hope couldn't have survived that week without us. No, we were there to meet her every need. And you know what, she flourished. I don't know if she exercised her faith to believe we would be there to provide care for her needs. I'm not going to take the analogy to extremes. But, she was put in a situation where she had no alternative but to be dependent on our care.

God allows situations to come into my life that force me to trust Him. To walk in faith is the goal of every person's life. To walk where you can't walk with your own strength. I have spent the good part of my life depending on my own strength and resources. I've come to the end of my strength and resources. Now I can live the *exciting life* that God has waiting for me. To be able to walk this way it takes an absence of fear and a measure of courage. I was never taught to live this way. I was not nurtured in the way of faith and courage. I'm not complaining by any means, in retrospect I realize that my past can pave the way to walk in faith and take courage in the fact that God can care for me. (*Haven't I commanded you: be strong and courageous? Do not be afraid or discouraged, for the Lord your God is with you wherever you go.* Joshua 1:9)

A couple of days before I fell from my nest and crashed to the ground, I found myself driving down a main street in San Clemente, California. I was stopped at a signal when a group of teenagers pulled up alongside of me. I was sitting there pondering the low point I was at in life. I thought, *I don't know how it could get any worse than this.*

Little did I know that in less than a week literally all hell was going to break loose and God was going to start me on a parallel journey of healing like Hope. On top of that I had just picked my nose (you know how some people do that when they are mindlessly waiting for the light to change).

Well, the teenagers in the car next to me were trying to get my attention so I would roll down my window. The girl that was sitting in the front passenger seat had a sheet of notebook paper folded into a little square. When I rolled down my window she yelled out to me to take the paper from her. My first thought was it's probably something stupid to make fun of me. My, how some old messages have a life of their own that just keep breathing on you.

I couldn't reach the paper so the driver told the girl, "Just throw it in his car." I thought, *She could never throw that from that distance and have it go through my window.* Frankly I had hoped she would miss so I could just drive off and not have to go through the temptation of reading something dumb that was intended to make fun of me.

She threw the paper. It went right through the window of my car and landed smack dab between my feet. I looked down and I couldn't believe it. The light changed, and the kids drove off. I reached down, picked up the paper, unfolded it and read the following words written with a big black marking pen.

I'M EXCITED
ABOUT YOUR
LIFE!!

"I'M EXCITED ABOUT YOUR LIFE"

I was completely undone emotionally. I had to pull over, and I just sobbed. Could God actually be speaking to me and does He care enough about me to use a group of teenagers in the middle of a weekday afternoon? Absolutely, and He would do the same for anyone else. He cares about every little detail of our lives and what we're going through.

Two weeks prior to that episode, I mindlessly drove through a red light with a policeman sitting at the intersection. I was once again dwelling on my stuff and definitely not trusting God. I was anxious about everything a person could be anxious about, and now I was pulling over and waiting for the policeman to give me a ticket. It was so obvious that I didn't have to wonder if he were going to pull me over. I had that sick feeling in my stomach familiar with going to the principal's office when I was young, fear that I had been found out.

The first words out of the officer's mouth were, "What were you thinking?" *Obviously I wasn't thinking about my driving*, that's for sure. What came out of my mouth was a shock to me, and I think the officer was shocked as well. I said, "Officer, I just can't take what's going on in my life right now. The company I work for is about to go out of business, and I think my marriage is over."

That was the first time I had verbalized anything about my marriage to any human being. In some weird way, I think it was some kind of a confession of truth that was allowing me to get back onto a path where God could start the healing process. Before I even finished the sentence, I just broke down crying.

My next thought was that the police officer must have been thinking, *nice try, buddy, but I'm still going to give you this ticket.* But it gets even better. On the dashboard of my car I had some herbal remedy that Nan had given me to make tea. This herbal remedy is a white powdered substance, and I had it in a plastic baggy.

Yep, I'm a smart one. I first of all pull over for the police officer and right there in plain sight is a plastic baggy with white powder in it. *Brilliant William, that is just brilliant.* Yes, you guessed it; the police officer's next question was real simple, "What's that in the baggy?"

I don't think I stuttered like that since I was fourteen when I asked a girl to go to the movies. I tried to explain to the officer what it was, but the more I spoke the worse it got. Finally, he rescued me from myself, and right in the middle of one of my stutter-filled sentences he plainly stated, "Give it to me."

He took the baggy to his squad car, and I just knew, *well, here I go. I'm going to jail and this time I may not get off so easily. And, Nan may not be willing to help me out this time. She may even say, "Well, that's what you deserve and I'm done with you anyway, so work it out yourself."* While all these thoughts were flooding through my mind, the officer appeared at my window once again. He said to me as he handed the baggy back to me. "Do yourself a favor and don't just leave that out in the open, someone could see that and think it's dope and break into your car to get it."

His next words shocked me, "I'm not going to ticket you. I'm just going to give you a warning, but you've got to *see the light.*" I didn't know how to even respond to this act of mercy. His final words were don't try to drive unless you can focus on what you're doing, and then he let me go. He let me go. In a weird way the officer's words set me free.

> I'm just going to give you a warning, but you've got to *see the light."*

I just sat there for the longest time and wept at the mercy that had been shown me, and the condition of my life. What's interesting about this story is that about a month before all this happened Nan had an unusual experience. While talking with her friend Katie on the phone Nan saw a picture in her mind of an anteater.

Katie happens to attend the University of California at Irvine. Nan asked her, "Isn't your school mascot an anteater?" Katie responded with, "Yes, it is." Nan asked her friend, "What's your school motto?" Katie said, "I don't know but let me check the Internet."

What she found was very interesting for a secular state university, she found the school motto: "*Let There Be Light.*" When Nan heard that, she said, "That's it. We've got to pray that God will send His light to Will." For the next month Nan had three of her friends praying that God would send His light to me.

I understand now that God desires to work behind the scenes on my behalf even when I don't have the desire to have Him working for me. God knows what I need before I can ask Him. There were times when Nan and I would be researching and looking for ways to take care of Hope. She wasn't even chirping or asking in her own way for us to meet her needs and take care of her. God is no different, and He has a heck of a lot more resources that we do.

Lesson 12:

The Love Boat

Wild hummingbirds have plenty of thoughts of food despite their minuscule brain, say researchers who note that the tiny birds' "episodic" memory for nectar feedings is so exact that it's unique among wildlife.

"Then Abram journeyed by stages to the Negev."
— **Genesis 12:9**

THIS MORNING I set out on a journey to walk three miles around the lake that's behind our house. I wanted to get some early morning exercise and just pray. The first two miles I was mostly just thanking God for the day and asking Him to bless me. I was just doing my thing to try to start the day out on a positive note. About three quarters of the way around the second lap, the thought came to me, *Why don't you just listen for a while?* So I just got quiet.

I walked for a few minutes being quiet (which is pretty amazing for me) when I came upon two women that were walking ahead of me. I could hear their conversation. I want to share the conversation that I heard from these two women that I affectionately call Laverne and Shirley. Their conversation was about what I have entitled the Love Boat.

Laverne and Shirley appeared to be in their early to mid-sixties. Laverne was sharing a conversation that she had with her husband about their boat. It went something like this.

Laverne: *"I told my husband that since he spends so much time with that old boat fixing the motor and making repairs on the boat, why doesn't he just buy a new boat?"* She went on to say, *"I told him before we get too old to enjoy going out on the boat, we should just spend the money and get something new and be able to enjoy our time, rather than spending so much time repairing the boat."* She continued, *"I asked him how much would a new boat cost?"*

She said her husband's response was, *"A new boat would be about thirty to thirty-five thousand dollars."* She said, *"I told him well why don't you just get a new boat?"* (I like Laverne a lot). Shirley chimed in with a wonderful British accent, *"Why yes, he should just get that boat, and the boys would love it as well."* Laverne responded, "You know my husband said, *'Well, the boys like to take the boat out fishing and when they fish they drop worms on the floor of the boat and step on them. They pretty much make a mess of the boat when they take it out. If we get a new boat, what are we going to do when the boys want to take it out and they make a mess of the new boat?'"*

Shirley spoke up and said, *"Yes and when you had your party, it was so wonderful to see the boys go down to the boat with their friends and sit in the boat during the party. It was like their own private lounge."* Laverne then said, "I told my husband, *you're right, how do we want the boys to remember us? Do we want them to remember us as parents, who were always saying, don't get that dirty, don't mess that up, and don't break anything? Or do we want them to remember us as always wanting them to come over and go out on the boat and have fun?*

So we decided not to get a new boat, were the final words I heard from Laverne as I walked ahead of them. I began to think about Laverne's boys. I thought about the memories that they could pass onto their children about the fun times on the boat. I thought about how Laverne and her husband might pass the boat on as an inheritance to the boys so their kids could make their own fun boat memories.

Then I began to think about my heavenly Father. How He has things stored up for me to enjoy as I journey through life. He, like Laverne, has no desire to be remembered as a Father that continually says "don't, don't, don't." No, He designs stages along the way of our journey in life that we can enjoy. Even when we are in stages that may be difficult, God is working to bring the best out of us, and the situation.

I wonder what memories Hope has in her journey. What conversations does she hear? I know that she doesn't have the capacity to listen to people and understand what they're saying. But can you imagine if she could, what she'd hear in the stages of her journey?

How much more does God want for us than what Laverne and her husband want for their boys? Could it be that God wants me to have fun? He wants me to enjoy life? Could it be true that when I make messes He isn't just waiting there to say, "Why did you do that?" No, I believe that God wants me to enjoy what He has given me because He loves me. He really is excited about my life!

Lesson 13:

Learning to Trust

I have a hummingbird trapped in my garage, what do I do?
In an hour, a trapped and exhausted hummingbird can
starve to death.

"Trust in the Lord with all your heart, Lean not on your own
understanding. In all your ways acknowledge Him and He
will direct your paths."

— **Proverbs 3: 5–6**

FEELING TRAPPED, NOT knowing what or who to trust—this is the toughest lesson of all. I've lived most of my life running from the pain of depression, and the fear of rage makes it difficult to trust anyone. Including God. Will He be there when I feel trapped? Will God help me out, or will I fall prey to hunger and exhaustion?

Hope has the innate ability to hunt for food. Hummingbird flight muscles make up more of their body weight than any other species of bird. They need these muscles for endurance to hunt for food. Hummingbirds burn calories at a faster rate than any other bird. They need food for fuel so they can fly and hunt for more food.

That's a lot like life, isn't it? I need strength everyday to get through the battles that I face. I need faith to fight discouragement. I need trust to fight the times of confusions that may come. I need hope to wait for the victories in life. Just because God has healed me of my depression doesn't mean I won't get discouraged or have thoughts that are negative. The difference now is that I have some "trust" muscles to go with the healing. When I do get a discouraging thought, I don't fall deep into a depressed state that debilitates me for an extended period of time. I'm learning that it's a daily discipline to seek help, wait for answers, and depend on God and others rather than isolate and allow the depression to win out. Sometime the most courageous choice I can make is to ask for help. Take the risk to be vulnerable with someone I trust. That's not easy and there's always the possibility that someone may reject me. That's okay that's how we grow up.

> Sometime the most courageous choice I can make is to ask for help. Take the risk to be vulnerable with someone I trust.

Big victories come by way of many *little* victories. Making choices to set my mind on good things is sometimes minute-by-minute. Getting up each morning and starting the day in prayer is a discipline now, not just a choice. I used to get up and take my medication for depression without thinking. Now I get up and go to my knees without thinking.

Psychologists would say that I'd have to be on antidepressants the rest of my life. My psychologists told me that *hundreds of times*. Each time I'd asked her, "Will I have to take my medications the rest of my life?" she would have the same answer: "Yes." Well, that didn't turn out to be true. I'm not advocating that anyone go off of antidepressants. What I am saying is God can heal mental illnesses just as easily as any physical illness.

Now I'm learning to retrain my mind. I call this "setting my mind on things above." Let me give an example of what I mean. I may hear the thought in my head that goes something like this: *You're not really healed, and you better go back on your medication.*

I can be deceived into believing that lie or I can trust the truth that situations and reactions are completely different for me since the moment that God touched me with His healing presence. No, I am healed, and now I'm learning daily how to live in the victory of my healing.

Some people believe that you can lose a healing from God if you allow doubt and unbelief back in. I personally don't know if that's true. I know that if I continue to trust that God is working on my behalf because He loves me, then I have nothing to worry about. My "trust" muscles are getting exercised and nourished every day. Trust comes with practice. Trust comes with practicing forgiveness.

> My "trust" muscles are getting exercised and nourished every day. Trust comes with practice. Trust comes with practicing forgiveness.

Forgiveness is the key to finding faith and trust in God and others. Just the other day, I slipped into some old ways of thinking and as a result Nan lost trust in me once again. Her lack of trust was merited because I responded to a situation the way I would have in the past by saying something that was negative about someone I didn't even know. Nan's response was, "I can't trust you in that area, and I should know better."

Her feelings were completely valid based on my behavior. Well, I stewed over this for the better part of a day. Finally, as we were driving to the store in silence, I said the magic words, "Nan, what I said earlier about [that person] was completely wrong and I hope you'll forgive me." Nan responded with, "I forgive you." I don't know if true forgiveness was received by Nan, it doesn't matter. What I learned was that it set me free. And trust will be rebuilt over time as I earn her trust.

Most of the day I had felt like I was in shackles again. When I asked for forgiveness, the freedom that came over me was incredible. Without forgiveness I can't have a relationship with God or people. It doesn't matter to me anymore if the person I ask for forgiveness from keeps holding the mistake against me. What matters is the freedom that comes through forgiveness. Asking Nan to forgive me for what I had said allowed me to enter back into prayer, allowed me to relax the rest of the day, and most importantly it allowed me to get back on track with writing.

> Without forgiveness I can't have a relationship with God or people.

I had planned on spending most of the day writing. When I opened my big mouth and said what I said about that person, I lost my joy and peace. I felt condemned and unworthy, disqualified to write or experience any of the life that comes with living in faith. I figured out yesterday a few things. I'm *still* healed. When I admit that I'm wrong (that's truth being exercised), freedom, trust, and faith are restored instantly.

If forgiveness were exercised more in relationships, there would be more unity and a heck of a lot fewer divorces. One night recently Nan and I walked to the store to pick up a few items. As we were walking out of the store, I glanced over to a magazine rack and there is actually a magazine called (get this) "Life After Divorce." I felt so much anger rise up in me. I hope it was righteous anger. I'm not judging anyone who gets divorced. That's not my point.

Both Nan and I have been divorced. I'm speaking from experience. In some situations divorce is merited. This is my point. Forgiveness is what makes relationships grow. Forgiveness is the key to restoration. Divorce can be an easy way out. It seems like divorce is such a viable option now days. It is difficult to work through the pain, but the benefits of forgiveness are beyond measure. Forgiveness builds faith and trust. Forgiveness is the foundation to the Christian life. When a person gives their life to Christ, they don't stop sinning. There's forgiveness waiting for me every single day, just like there'll always be another flower waiting for Hope to find for food.

This maybe the toughest lesson to learn, but I think it just might have the greatest reward. Listen to this interaction between Jesus and Peter.

* * *

"Take this most seriously: A yes on earth is yes in heaven; a no on earth is no in heaven. What you say to one another is eternal. I mean this. When two of you get together on anything at all on earth and make a prayer of it, my Father in heaven goes into action. And when two or three of you are together because of me, you can be sure that I'll be there." At that point Peter got up the nerve to ask, "Master, how many times do I forgive a brother or sister who hurts me? Seven?" Jesus replied, "Seven! Hardly. Try seventy times seven."

— (Matthew 18:20–22, The Message).

* * *

What's interesting is Jesus said first, "Where two or three are gathered together." There's unity in that statement. What destroys unity? Unforgiveness destroys unity. Then Jesus goes on to tell Peter that basically you'll never reach a place where you don't have to forgive. "As long as we both shall live [under one roof], I will ask forgiveness."

I think I learned something from this whole forgiveness experience that'll lead me to a place of deeper trust. I believe in the power of forgiveness today, it brings life. I imagine little Hope flying from flower to flower drinking in nectar that gives her life. Forgiveness is the nectar of my life.

Learning to trust comes through forgiveness. God forgives me when I ask Him. When I believe the truth of God's forgiveness in my life, I'm then able to forgive myself and trust my relationship with Him. That trust then branches out to those I love. Could it be that I'm beginning to love myself? Could forgiveness be the way to trust that God really does love me? And could it be that God's love for me allows me to fly on the wings of trust?

I had a dream recently where I was at a party and everyone was introducing himself or herself. I was in a group of four men standing together and each of the men extended their hand and said, *I'm Joe, I'm John, I'm Jack.* When it came to my turn I shook the other men's hands and said, *I'm forgiven.*

When I woke up from the dream I thought *that's who I am*, that's my identity. I'm not a doctor, or a Pastor or on and on. I'm not even William, *I'm forgiven.* And if I'm forgiven I now have the ability to forgive. Think about that for a while. I then went crazy with this whole concept and thought I'm not only forgiven, but I'm loved, I'm happy, I'm hope, (well maybe not I'll leave that tag for our little hummingbird friend. Who are you? What do you hear God referring to you as?

Lesson 14:

Eight Days to a Miracle

HERE'S WHAT HAPPENED. We found Hope on a Sunday, and on the following Sunday we gave her to the Lisa Birkle, Assistant Director of the Wetlands Bird Estuary. Eight days. That's all the time we had with that little bird, but it sure did have a lasting impact on me. Those days will forever be my eight days to a miracle. My eight days of re-creation.

I cried out to God for years, "Take this rage from me. Why won't you heal me? What have I done wrong?" "Please forgive me God". Years spent in hidden places crying to God for Him to come and change me. Circumstances seemed to always rule over me and cause this ugly reaction to occur, rage. Then something happened.

I woke up one morning and I couldn't do life anymore. I asked for help, and there was help. It was Friday, June 13. Doug Webster, pastor of Lake Hills Community Church, a dear friend with a sincere desire to help people in need, came during his busy schedule and prayed with all his heart. Eight days of Nan and I getting real with each other, tears, honesty, forgiveness.

I started to meet with Kirk Peterman of Red Oaks Prayer and Healing Ministry. He prayed for me every Thursday for months. He prayed for deliverance and healing. It was a process of healing just like the eight days that Hope spent with us. We fed her in the morning, changed her water, and fed her again and again. We kept her in a safe place the best we knew how. Then we got her to the expert (Lisa).

Kirk Peterman was the expert in my life. He provided safety for me. He provided friendship. He was a support system. Some days he really let me have it with a good dose of honesty. Other days he just sat with me in silence as God's peace ministered to me. He provided the structure I needed to facilitate healing. He taught me. He didn't judge me. And he surely didn't try to fix me. He left that up to God.

Kirk taught me about receiving God's love. He taught me about trusting God and Him alone. He taught me how to fight, and how to rest. He spoke to me about God's grace, and letting go. Kirk was a sounding board. He was a confidante. He was used like an instrument in God's hand.

The irony to my healing is that God used my wife to heal me. She was the one person who was hurt the most from my depression and rage, the one person who had the most right to turn her back on me and reject me. God moved through the prayers of my wife and literally through her hands. Nan may not have had any love left for me, but the compassion that God placed in her heart moved her to pray.

The healing took place one night in bed. Nan was praying over me and specifically for my brain. I don't remember any of her words. I just remember what I felt and heard. As she was praying, the left side of my brain became extremely warm and tingling. This warm tingling sensation lasted for quite a while. As Nan continued to pray, I reached out and grabbed her hand and placed it on the left side of my head.

A few seconds after Nan had placed her hand on my head, I heard a click in my head. It was a shifting of something in my brain, like tumblers in a lock lining up. My brain just clicked into place. Then the warm tingling sensation on the left lobe of my brain continued for several more seconds. Was God balancing out the chemicals that were out of balance? I don't know but I felt and heard the *click*.

The next morning I felt a deep conviction in my soul that it would be wrong for me to take my antidepressant medication. I actually had the thought that if I took the antidepressants that morning they would make me sick. A battle in my head lasted for a few minutes. The thought came to me; *you better call your psychiatrist before you stop taking your medication.* Then I thought, *But where's your faith?* I knew that something had happened. I heard the clicking and felt the shifting in my brain. I felt that warm tingling sensation. I made the decision to not take the antidepressants that morning.

I haven't taken any since. Do I get depressed? No more than anyone else. I have sad thoughts, but they don't keep me down for days at a time. No, I'm healed. God did a miracle for me. It's a pretty simple story with incredible results. The people in my life who really know me are amazed. I can tell by their questions from time to time that they're wondering if this is going to last. I think that's pretty normal. But the truth is life gets better with time. I can feel life settling into a routine of decision-making and trust that becomes more consistent with each day that passes.

> God did a miracle for me. It's a pretty simple story with incredible results.

My path may be different than others, but I know that God wants us to be well. He wants to fulfill our destiny. God doesn't want the enemy of our soul to win out. He wants us to live in freedom. God did hear the cry of my heart to be well.

He heard the cry of my heart for "destiny fulfilled." Is this a miracle? You bet it is!

When I think back on those eight days that we spent with that little hummingbird and all the details that were handled, I understand a little better about how God works, how God is in the little details to make big things happen. God desires me to experience Him in a great big way as I face situations that life brings my way. There will be difficulty in life. That's just part of life but I don't have to fall captive to circumstances. I can trust that God will be with me through the difficult times of life. I can now walk in peace.

In eight days I was able to start life over and have a new beginning to my life. I was given the opportunity to learn how to navigate through the storms of life with help. I don't have to isolate anymore. The old patterns of doing life are no longer a viable option. I'm learning to depend on others for help. And especially God, who is my Help. Trusting Him is my job now.

Eight days, and now I know that God is my redeemer. These are no longer just words that I spew forth. No, God is my redeemer. He is redeeming my dreams: dreams of a healthy marriage, dreams of ministry, dreams of relationships restored. Dreams do come true when God redeems.

My story is quite simple. It's just like Hope coming into our lives. God just showed up one day and said, "It's time." God did it. He healed me and continues to bring experiences my way so I can live in faith, trusting that He will take me where He's always planned for me to go. My story is that God's promises are true. Do they look the way I thought they would? Absolutely not, but I can say I wouldn't have it any other way. I'm now excited about my life.

My story is that God's promises are true.

Kirk asked me the other day to pray and ask God why He made me. Kirk went on to share his story about how one day his mentor asked him this very powerful question: "Kirk what do you want?" Kirk said before he could even form a thought, the word, "pastor" came out of his mouth. After Kirk shared this story with me, we spent the rest of the session in silence. The silence became peace to me.

I've been plagued with the question, "God, why did You put me here on earth and what did You create me for?" It has been the question that has almost destroyed me on numerous occasions over the years. The enemy of my soul would say that I'm useless. I have no worth. I'm good for nothing. All lies. They're all lies. The truth is God has a plan for me. He has wonderful plans for every creature on earth. None of us is useless in the eyes of God Almighty.

I left Kirk's office, and the peace I'd felt stayed with me as I got into my car to drive home—peace that went beyond my understanding, peace that spoke deep inside of me that "everything is going to be okay."

At this moment (it's Saturday morning), I'm at peace when I type these next words—the words that answer the question, "What do you want, Will?"

I want to spend the rest of my life writing books that will change people's lives. I want to spend the rest of my life teaching people how to trust God for healing and deliverance in their lives. I want to travel all over the world ministering in the healing presence of God. I, too, like Kirk, want to pastor again. I want to pastor a church with Nan and me teaching/preaching side-by-side most Sundays. I will say it now for the first time in public, "I'm a writer, teacher/pastor."

That felt great!

There I laid it out there, my life vision on paper. You can, too. I'm not afraid of people's reactions to what I want. I won't worry about my qualifications or lack of qualifications. You see, I'm no longer disqualified. I'm not bound by the lies of the enemy about my soul that would try to tell me that depression or rage has disqualified me. Nope, I know what I want, and God, if He wills, can make it happen. And to think that all it took was spending eight days with Hope. What a miracle. Peace. Deep peace that goes way past my understanding of what's reality. I choose to live in peace.

I now choose faith and faith alone. I trust that God is moving behind the scenes to do a miracle for me just like He did for Hope during those eight days. I know that it's no harder for God to fulfill plans in a person's life than it is to heal the sick, deliver people from the demonic, or for that matter take care of a little hummingbird that has lost its way.

Even as I write these words, I can feel the doubt try to creep back in. What thoughts must have plagued Noah when God asked him to build an ark? No rain in sight, no thunder or lightning, just the sound of people laughing while he hammered away in faith. Was it Noah's faith in his ability to build an ark? No, it was Noah's faith in God and God alone.

Lesson 15:

Tendencies

Hummingbirds can fly right, left, up, down, backwards, and even upside down. While other birds get their flight power from the down-stroke only, hummingbirds gain strength on the up-stroke as well.

*T*ENDENCIES, NOW THAT'S an interesting word. Hummingbirds have some real interesting tendencies when it comes to flying that are inbred. They are unique in terms of their ability to fly and the way they can maneuver their wings. Why is it that hummingbirds possess these unique tendencies? Why can't other birds fly upside down, vertically and backwards like hummingbirds? Could it be that hummingbirds, because of their lack of size, have to make up for it with maneuverability?

While Hope was cooped up in her cage, she didn't have the space available to practice all of her flight moves. Her ability to fly was limited to the space available in the cage. She may never have been able to develop her potential had she been left in her cage. Her ability to fly probably would have stayed limited to what she was familiar with within the confines of her cage.

I've noticed recently that some of my tendencies are growing as I extend out in this newfound place of healing. How I responded to situations in the past doesn't really work anymore. It feels "awkward" to me, awkward in that I respond to a situation then find myself sort of correcting myself in mid-flight knowing that there is more that I have to offer in a situation than that to which I'm accustomed.

This has caused some conflict in relationships. Here's an example. Nan might ask me about something, expecting one of my old responses. When she questions me about why I responded the way I did, most of the time I don't know why I responded that way but it feels good. It feels right. It feels more authentic. My thought is, *I didn't know my wings could fly that way.* My next thought is, *why did I respond that way?* It's like my brain is reprogramming itself without me being involved.

It's got to be like the first few times Hope flew outside of her cage and discovered it was more efficient to fly backward and to the right to get to a flower. She realized that was the first time she had performed that flight pattern. After a few times it became a natural tendency for her. She can now fly any way she wants without thinking about it.

Here's another example. I've always wanted to pray with Nan. In the past I felt that if we prayed together she would be critiquing my prayers, asking me questions like why I prayed a certain way or what did I mean when I prayed that way. Or what would really upset me was when she prayed with a "sermon in mind" to drive the point home to me. I would get angry and leave all upset, and our prayer time would be ruined.

Eventually like everything else in our marriage we just stopped praying together. It bothered me that we couldn't pray together. I knew it was my tendency to sabotage our prayer time. Why would I do that? I'm not sure. Maybe fear was at the root.

I tend to initiate our prayer time now. If Nan begins to pray something that I may not agree with or when I don't understand her motive, my tendency is to quiet my spirit and just listen. I listen while she talks to God. Sometimes I feel like its just Nan and God in the room, and I get the privilege of listening in. If I can hear Nan's heart, then I find myself being less judgmental. It becomes more natural the more we pray. It's becoming a part of who I am. My natural tendency has changed when it comes to praying with Nan.

Tendencies can be a source of my greatest struggles. Who am I really, what is my real personality? These are questions that I find myself seeking the answer to on a daily basis. The answers come in bits and pieces. Patience is a part of this process, and patience is something I haven't been real good at in the past.

When Hope was released, I wonder if she just sat there for a moment and tried to figure out where in the world she was. She was completely free without any walls or ceiling to hold her back. Did she just take off? I don't think so. I'm sure that her world grows each and every day as she navigates through her day. She probably learns something new that becomes a valuable part of who she's becoming in the "brave new world."

In the last month, different people have told me that I have to learn to wrestle with God to understand just how much He loves me. I have to wrestle with Him so I can trust Him. I don't really know what's true when it comes to this "wrestling stuff." I do know that today I woke up and realized that I could just surrender. That's right just throw up the old white flag.

Quitting has always been a difficult concept for me to grasp. My tendency is to fight too long and wear out everyone involved, or quit prematurely and fear that I've missed out on the benefits of hanging in a bit longer. Pride sometimes gets in the way as well. I tend to have to get the last word in no matter what the cost.

This morning I was driving to work, and I said out loud, "God, I give up. I'm not wrestling with you anymore." I had a picture in my mind of me just lying on the ground and saying, "Go ahead, God, pin me, you win. One, two, three, there you pinned me, and you win." That's what I want anyway. I want God to win out in my life, and I want to surrender my life to His will.

Maybe this will be a new tendency for me. The way I view what happened today was that I was saying, "God, I trust you. You can pin me because I know You won't hurt me. I can trust You; I learned a new way to fly." Hummingbirds can fly vertically. That makes them unique. What I'm learning about myself is that I have some tendencies that make me unique as well.

> "God, I trust you. You can pin me because I know You won't hurt me. I can trust You; I learned a new way to fly."

"When the going gets tough, the tough surrender and say, 'Help, God, show me the way.'" That's the tendency I want foremost in my life. I want to trust God above my circumstances. I understand that there are times we have to wrestle through things in prayer. But here's the difference with what happened "today." When it's time to surrender and I'm sure it is, I need to quit fighting and just give up and trust God.

Here's the lesson learned regarding *tendencies*. Before when I would read my Bible, pray, or perform any other act of service to God it felt more like a duty to try and get my way or just be religious. I didn't enjoy it all (honestly, I hated it); they seemed like just religious acts. The past few weeks I've been thinking, *how much can I pray or read my Bible before I can get to a place of not having to wrestle with God?* This morning I realized I don't have to do any of that stuff. God is already pleased with me.

I pray because I want to seek God and know Him and His ways. The same with reading the Bible I don't have to be looking for a sermon in everything I read, or read the Bible as a religious duty. I can just read the Bible out of the sheer enjoyment of getting to know God a little better.

I find myself praying and reading the Bible more. If it's like all the other tendencies that are a part of who I'm becoming, I'll be doing a lot of praying and reading. After all, it's what I tend to do.

One last lesson learned on tendencies. Since I've received healing and deliverance, I've found that I have a bent toward drawing. I mean I can draw faces and actually do it well. I think it must've been some latent talent in me that got ripped off when I was young. I do remember winning some art contest in elementary school. There's something about drawing that has become very easy for me. More importantly, it's enjoyable. When I feel anxious or stressed, I find myself wanting to draw. It relaxes me.

I bring the issue of drawing up because I think this is an important aspect of healing that sometimes is overlooked. Darkness comes to shroud light. Darkness keeps people from seeing what really is or the ability to see clearly. In my case, it was the fact that anxiety would overwhelm me and become fear. The fear would cause me to isolate. When someone would try to break into my isolation, I would become angry and eventually rage would take over.

This dark cycle would keep me from becoming who I was meant to be and also keep me from being in relationships. Now that the shroud of darkness has been removed, I'm finding things out about myself that I never knew resided within me. Like the drawing it just bubbled up in me one day. I wanted to draw. I began to see things in my mind as I was waking up in the morning or as I drifted off to sleep. I could see the detail of someone's nose or eyes.

I have found that I have an ability to draw portraits. This talent was inspired from within me. Now I look at people differently. I look at the uniqueness of their features. It has allowed me to see people differently.

Viewing things in this new way also happens with seeing nature. I see the colors in the trees and flowers differently. I look at the details of animals, cats and dogs for example. The world has come alive and it makes each day more exciting. I get inspiration from places, people, and things that I see like never before.

When healing and deliverance takes place in a person's life, it's for a reason. It is to set people free to become the person that God designed. People can begin to see clearer. This is called vision. For me, I'm seeing a whole new vision. Not a version of the old vision, but an ability to look and see what is new for me today.

It's an exciting way to live. Desires that were never there before begin to bubble up. I want to go dancing with Nan. I want to create with whatever venue that's presented to me, whether it's drawing or music or writing poetry, even cooking. Or, even a business idea. Deliverance from the darkness has allowed me to see a view from where I stand today that is exciting. I look at people living their lives and wonder what talent is in them waiting to come out. Like I said before, drawing is relaxing. It's not only relaxing, but sometimes when I'm drawing I'll get inspiration for something else. An idea breaks into my thoughts.

The drawing puts me in a place of rest that allows me to receive inspiration. I've heard other people talk about how the arts affect them in this way. I never understood it before. Now I understand. It makes sense that a God who is the Creator of all things would want us to experience the joy of creating and meet us in that place to bring inspiration. It's actually kind of therapeutic.

Speaking of therapeutic, it's important to address the subject of re-entry into who I am or better yet, who I am becoming. There is this awkwardness about who I am right now. I find myself not really comfortable with the old Will and not knowing how the new Will is going to respond (or for that matter who the new Will is).

For most of my adult life I've struggled with what I believed to be a "call on my life" from God. I'm not sure what the call is or how it would be fulfilled. I had this sense that I was made to do something special. The frustration that comes with the call not being fulfilled creates a lot of strife in my marriage. I tend to get so self-absorbed with trying to figure out why I was put here on earth that Nan becomes "worn out" with the constant attention that I give this dilemma.

I've tried over the years all the "stuff" that the church suggests doing. I even went out and planted a church without any formal training. Our denomination holds the philosophy that you go out and plant (start) a church, and if it lasts it's of God. It went well for a few years and then, like I shared before, rage and depression took over and the rest is history.

There were times when I was preaching/teaching that made me feel fulfilled. We'd be driving home after church on Sunday, and I would share with Nan something like, "Gosh you know today when I was preaching I felt that this is what I was made to do." I wouldn't get much response from Nan. Maybe it was because she knew Monday was coming, which was known as "blue Monday" around our house.

I also found out from Nan recently that she never really got much from my teaching style. She just couldn't receive the message with all the stuff that went on between us. Who can blame her? Getting to the core of issues and moving forward to heal our marriage can be brutal sometimes. But I would rather have it this way then continue living a lie.

Anyway, this is what I surrendered to God this week. I released "the call" to Him. I just want to be a "regular guy." If He wants to do something with me than that would be great.

If not, then I asked him to help me to be just a regular guy living life to its fullest. I came to this conclusion after Nan and I had an argument over the same old topic. "What did God make me for?"

Nan said to me, "I don't understand why you can't be a regular guy, happy go lucky." Those words stayed with me through the rest of the evening. I didn't really sleep well and kept both of us up most of the night. Early in the morning, I grabbed my Bible and my journal and walked out to the lake behind our house. I read for a while—prayed some, too. Then I began to write a poem.

The poem is entitled "A Regular Guy." In writing this poem I felt for some reason like I was able to come to grips with the fact that God is in control. It allowed me to get back in to the present and enjoy what I have in front of me today. So I threw up the white flag and said, "God you win. From now on I'm going to practice staying in today, being a regular guy just doing 'happy.' My new mantra with Nan is, I'm a regular guy just doin' happy. God give me grace.

Regular Guy

The passions gone, dreams released, I'm movin' on, just
findin' my peace.
Yes, I'm movin' on, to find my way, just doin' happy, will
be okay.
Regular guy, just havin' fun, happy go lucky, on the run.
That's me now regular guy, a regular wife, livin' no lie.
Makin' life tough is a passin' fancy, makin' it easy, lovin'
Nancy.
Nothin' big, nothin' grand, just want to be regular
brand.
Regular guy havin' lots of fun, happy go lucky, no need
to be one.
That's me now regular guy, a regular life no shirt or tie.
I was young, a dream in hand, now I'm primed to take
my stand.
The status quo can now be mine, a regular guy is mighty
fine.
Enjoyin' life and havin' fun, walkin' the lake, feelin' the
sun.
I'll say a few prayers on my way, round again just another
day.
I'm excited 'bout life, cause there's no strife.
No angry burn, no waiting my turn.
Regular guy just havin' fun, happy go lucky, laughin' a
ton.
That's me now regular guy, a regular life give it a try.

— William Cuccia

Lesson 16:

The Prisoner Set Free

Now it was the governor's custom at the Feast to release a
prisoner chosen by the crowd.
— Matthew 27:15

I FIND MYSELF GETTING quiet in situations, weighing what I'm going to say in my mind and listening for what's going on inside of me. I'm practicing this more and more. But, it raises some questions for me. I feel like a prisoner who has been released from jail after serving a thirty-year sentence. Think about all the adjustments I would have to make after being incarcerated for that length of time. Being in prison for that long would definitely cause a person to have developed some habits that need to change.

In 1978, the average price of a car was $6,379. The average price for a gallon of milk was $1.44. A loaf of bread 32 cents, and a stamp 15 cents. And get this—the average home cost $62,500. And finally let me break your heart with this fun little fact about 1978. A gallon of gas cost (are you sitting down?) 62 cents.

Not to mention that the Blues Brothers made their first appearance on *Saturday Night Live*. The first test-tube baby was born (Louise Brown, July 25, 1978). Jimmy Carter was President. And the movie *Grease* was a box office hit.

Now let's jump ahead to the present day, 2008. I get healed and delivered, and the way I've been doing my adult life for the last thirty years no longer works. There is some adjusting that needs to take place for everyone with whom I have relationship. I just can't walk out the gates of the prison that has been my home for the past thirty years and expect everyone to just adjust to my coming-out party. What? Gas now costs almost four bucks a gallon? Are you kidding me?

No, first off, I have to learn how the present world works. What's going on in the world? How do I live in this new millennium? This is a process that I think about each and every time I ponder where Hope is and how she is doing. I know I've mentioned this before, but I wonder what Hope did the first time she was set free. I mean, when she was totally free, no more coming back to the aviary. Did she just take off, or did she have some sort of adjustment period to experiencing complete freedom?

I'm finding that I have a lot of adjusting to do. Situations that were familiar to me tend to feel awkward now. All of a sudden I'm an adult with little experience in a situation even though I've experienced it many times before.

For the past thirty years, my experience is from within the prison walls of depression and rage. So now when I'm in a situation, it's like I'm experiencing it for the first time. At times I'll experience some level of joy, and then moments later I may feel sadness. I'm sad because I think about everything that was missed. Not just for me, but also for loved ones and friends. Depression and rage contributed to a lot of people being ripped off of experiences that could have been much more enjoyable and profitable.

I realize I can't change the past. I've got to move forward. That doesn't mean the past won't still come up and rear its ugly head. Even though I can't control or change situations, that's not going to keep me from trying to make good choices and develop new ways of communicating. Relationships are much more valuable now.

Because of this newfound value in relationships, I find myself panicking from time to time. I panic that Nan is still going to leave me if I make a mistake. I panic that I'll never be able to be a productive person in the workplace if I'm not perfect. These are all lies that are a part of my thirty-year prison experience. Most days I can get to a place and realize, "Wait a minute, I'm not in prison anymore. I'm free to experience life in a fresh new way."

Here's an example of how communication affects relationships. Nan and I drive down to the harbor in Dana Point to have a picnic dinner and to go for a walk. As we drive down to the harbor, we take a detour through San Juan Capistrano where we used to live. As we pass by a local restaurant that's known for its peach pie (which is Nan's favorite), Nan asks, "I wonder when the peach pie season ends?" My response is, "I thought peach season is in the fall." My wife's reply is, "No, the fall is rhubarb, pumpkin, and—" I interrupt her, "—and apple pie." "Yes," she says, "and apple pie."

Now here's where the old and the new get really muddy. My next statement is, "We should take a trip to Julian this fall and get apple pie." I think it would be fun and romantic to get dressed up in warm autumn clothes and drive out to the mountain area of Julian where they grow apples and are known for their apple "goodies." Great idea right? Wrong. Listen to what Nan's response is. "You're kidding right? You hate Julian, you never wanted to go to Julian before."

Nan's next statement is even more telling. "I don't even know who you are. Who is this man? Are you just saying this because you think that's what I want to hear?" I laugh, because remember I'm just a *regular guy, doin' happy*. Then I respond with, "No, when I thought of apple pie, my next thought was not, *Gee, I wonder what Nan wants to hear right now*. Actually, my thought was, *wouldn't it be fun to go to Julian for apple pie and ice cream?* It sounded fun and romantic." I finish with, "Sweetheart, I'm just sharing the facts with you, that's all. It just sounded like it would be fun."

Nan looks at me a little confused and says, "Well, doesn't it seem a little weird to you that you would want to go Julian and do something like that?" I have to admit, "Yes, it does but I'm not trying to figure out why, I just know it's what I would like to do."

What was great about this interaction was we actually talked without it escalating into to some act of rage on my part. That felt good. Really good!

These conversations happen all the time now and not just with Nan. It happens with other people who know me. They may not be as aware of the change like Nan, but I can see them wondering why's Will responding the way he is. Everyone including me expects the voice and attitudes of the "prisoner" to break forth. Sometimes I just don't know what to do with what's going on inside of me.

Everything around me is different; my feelings and responses are different. After all, I've been healed, and it makes sense when I really think about it. A prisoner who has been in jail for thirty years is going to react to the environment around him much differently when he gets out. It's thirty years down the road, and everything has changed including the prisoner.

There are patterns so ingrained in me from the years of rage and depression that my mind automatically goes into some type of auto-response to situations. What's different is I don't always react to the situations like I used to. Think about the prisoner who lives in a five-foot by eight-foot cell for eighteen hours or more a day for twenty or thirty years. When he goes to sleep at night in a regular bedroom, it's going to feel a little bit strange. That five-by-eight foot cell is the prisoner's security.

I heard the story of an ex-convict who wanted to build a house with a five-foot by eight-foot cell so that at any time he could go in that cell and find security. I can't imagine why anyone would want to do something like that. If they had the opportunity to build a home for themselves, why would they want to have a memory of the past like that be a part of their new home? Just because it's familiar, it represents safety, that doesn't make it right.

Well, the more I thought about that, the more I realized how our behaviors are no different. When I get scared, I want to run and hide. Like when I was that little four-year-old hiding under that bed, or under the turtle at the park. When that comes over me, I know now hiding's not a viable option. I know it's not healthy. The difference now is I have new awareness of what is healthy, and I can choose. That's right, I can choose *just doin' happy.*

Before, I would just react to the rage or depression and believe that the only safe place was isolation. That way I couldn't hurt anyone and they couldn't hurt me. I see now how that mentality kept me in the prisoner role. So now when situations come up and I think I'll just run and hide, it doesn't feel right to me. That's not healthy. Why am I wanting to run and hide? What's happening that's causing that old response to come up?

The jailor doesn't want us to get free. He wants to keep us in bondage. He wants us to get comfortable in our five-by-eight prison cells. He wants us to desire to keep a place in our lives where we can fall back on the old ways of behaving like the ex-con who wanted to have a prison cell built in his new home. It's just a big lie. The truth is God set me free and allowed me to walk right out of that prison of depression and rage, and He never wants me to go back.

Nan and I were talking tonight about the new home that we're praying God is going to give her to replace the home in San Juan Capistrano. I told her, "I hope God does, because I don't want to go to my grave without a reprieve." Nan said, "What do you mean?" My response was, "I want God to make up for that mistake I made." Nan's next statement harpooned me.

She said, "God has forgiven you, and He's forgotten. He doesn't hold that stuff against us. And I've forgiven you, too. I miss that house and the things that went with it, but just because I miss and talk about it doesn't mean I don't forgive you." I was stunned. That statement made forgiveness take on a whole new meaning for me. It just gave me another rung on the "freedom ladder" for me to take another step upward in the healing process. And the reality is I couldn't get that house back or buy a new home for Nan in and of my own ability or resources. That's the beauty of being set free.

> Nan's next statement harpooned me. She said, "God has forgiven you, and He's forgotten. He doesn't hold that stuff against us. And I've forgiven you, too.

A prisoner just doesn't get out of prison after thirty years and take up where he left off. No, there's an adjustment period, for some longer than others. Some don't adjust and end up going back to what they know, prison life. The difference with God healing a person is that when God does something, it is done. And I mean done. I don't have to be in a hurry to get everything right.

The "jailor" tries to get us to buy into the lies that we're really not healed or that we aren't any different. But with each new day, the power of the lie is less effective. And with each situation that has a different response comes a confidence in what God has done.

It really is about forgiveness more and more. The more I can forgive myself and accept God's forgiveness, the greater the distance becomes between the walls of the prison and me. I wonder where Hope is. I wonder if she has gained the confidence to fly somewhere really far. I'm sure she has no intention to fly anywhere near the aviary where she was released. She probably has no desire to be caged up again after experiencing what freedom feels like.

There's a Bible character named Joseph. He was one of the twelve sons of Israel. He was the favored son. His father even gave him a special coat of many colors that made his older brothers jealous. What made matters worse is that Joseph had a couple of dreams in which his brothers and parents bowed to him. When the opportunity arose, Joseph's brothers had planned on dumping him in an empty cistern and leave him there to die. Judah (one of Joseph's older brothers) had a change of heart and talked the other brothers into selling Joseph to some Midianite merchants that were passing by. The Midianites took Joseph to Egypt.

Joseph than becomes the most powerful man in all of Egypt with the exception of Pharaoh (his boss). Years later in the middle of a famine the brothers go to Egypt for help. Through a series of encounters with Joseph (whom the brothers don't recognize at first), they are reunited. Joseph reveals himself to his brothers, and it's very emotional to say the least. The display of forgiveness that Joseph shows his brothers is incredible.

* * *

Then he threw his arms around his brother Benjamin and wept, and Benjamin embraced him, weeping. And he kissed all his brothers and wept over them. Afterward his brothers talked with him.

— Genesis 45:14–15

* * *

"And Joseph kissed all his brothers." When I read that recently I could relate to what the brothers must have felt. To think that my wife would forgive me and that God has kept her for me is a great miracle. I feel like I've been kissed and blessed by God, kissed with His forgiveness and healing power. When forgiveness and healing take place it just like getting kissed from God with the most endearing kiss.

Forgiveness
Genesis 45:15

I've been kissed; yes I've been blessed.
Somehow You made a way,
Without a word, without a glare,
You did not look the other way.

I've been kissed; yes I've been blessed.
Somehow You found a way,
Without guilt, without shame
You found no need to repay.

I've been kissed; yes I've been blessed.
Somehow You chose a way,
Without disdain, without regret
Your forgiveness paid my debt.

I've been kissed; yes I've been blessed.
With Your forgiveness I've been kissed.

— William Cuccia

Lesson 17:

Torpor

Torpid hummingbirds exhibit a slumber that is as deep as death. In 1832, Alexander Wilson first described hummingbird torpor in his book, American Ornithology; "No motion of the lungs could be perceived ... the eyes were shut, and, when touched by the finger, [the bird] gave no signs of life or motion."

"NO SIGNS OF life or motion," now that's encouraging. Sounds like death to me. And that's exactly what it is. Let me say it this way, "For to me, to live is Christ and to die is gain" (Philippians 1:21). To die is gain. I had to die to all my dreams, and I'm glad. I had to die to what I thought was the life that God had for me and slip into torpor. Deep rest. It's in that place of rest where life comes forth with energy. It called inspiration.

Recently I've been practicing slow, deep breathing. My sophomore year in high school, I took biology. My biology teacher Mr. Resnick had us do an experiment in lab one day where we had to breathe into a bag and then hold our breath for as long as we could. I played every sport made available to me since the time I was six years old. So I put myself into the athlete category for the lab test.

When it was my turn to take the test I went for it. Being competitive I thought, "I'm going to hold my breath longer than anyone in the class." Well, I took my breaths into the brown paper bag, and when my teacher said, "Go," I held my breath. And I held my breath and held my breath. I held my breath for a full forty-five seconds.

When I finally started to breathe again, you would have thought someone had been holding me under for twenty minutes. I was gasping for air while all my basketball buddies were laughing their heads off. My performance placed me in the category with the "smokers" in the class. Most of the athletes were able to hold their breath for at least a minute and a half.

Needless to say practicing slow, deep breathing has been very beneficial for me. It is very relaxing and tends to wash away any anxiety. This is similar to what a hummingbird does to preserve its energy.

Even when hummingbirds are sleeping, they have huge metabolic demands that must be met simply to survive the night when they can't forage. To meet this energetic challenge, hummingbirds save enough energy to survive cold nights by lowering their internal thermostat at night, becoming hypothermic.

Torpor is a type of deep sleep where a hummingbird lowers its metabolic rate by as much as ninety-five percent. A torpid hummingbird consumes up to fifty times less energy when torpid than when awake. This lowered metabolic rate also causes a cooled body temperature. A hummingbird's nighttime body temperature is held at a hypothermic threshold that is barely sufficient to maintain life. This threshold is known as their *set point*, and it is far below the normal daytime body temperature of 104°F or 40°C recorded for other similarly-sized birds.

Hmmm, fifty times less energy used in torpor. Now that sounds like something of value. Most of my adult life I've felt like my heartbeat was going at 1,260 beats per minute—just racing all the time. Taking time to slow things down and get some real rest has so many benefits. The first noticeable effect after I was free from depression and rage was a total absence of my mind racing. For a couple of days, there was just quiet in my head. Usually I have what seems like ten different thoughts competing for my attention, which causes a high degree of anxiety (and shallow breathing I might add). That's gone now.

I still have anxiety, but it would be considered normal for the situation. I don't live with it constantly anymore. One Saturday, for example, Nan and I were driving to this area we'd never been to before. To get there, we had to drive on a road of mountain switchbacks that was narrow and had no guardrails. About every couple of miles there were signs that read, "Caution, extreme drop offs." That experience was a bit anxiety provoking. That type of experience would make anyone anxious.

For Hope, torpor allows her to save energy, energy she'll need to be able to hunt for food or to fend off a predator. Reserve energy is a valuable asset. In the past I've tended to run on empty most of the time, and that makes me vulnerable emotionally and compromises the immune system. Getting rest is beyond a necessity. When rested, I'm able to think more clearly and respond rather than react to a situation. There's also an absence of anxiety when I'm at rest.

In torpor, a hummingbird's body temperature is reduced and/or placed in a cooling state. I found this interesting. "A cooling state," or taking time to cool off, allows the body and emotions to rebuild. Sometimes it's better to remove myself from a situation to "cool off" and take some time to think about what really happened. This "cooling off" period is healing to my soul. It can be invigorating, like when I jump into a cold shower or the ocean during winter.

The other evening, Nan and I were down at the beach swinging on some swings. It was an evening of torpor in a way, just relaxing on the swings taking in the sunset. All of a sudden I had the urge to run down to the water and get my feet wet. It was cold. But after a couple of minutes my feet adjusted to the water temperature, and it felt invigorating. Even as we were walking back to the car, the cool temperature of my feet brought energy to my whole body. I had renewed energy even though it was the end of a long day.

Seasons of rest allow for the mind, body, and soul to be energized so that when the energy is needed I have something to offer. People who have a bent toward depression and/or rage tend to run on empty all the time. It's like the internal mechanism that tells us it's time for torpor doesn't work. Experiences from our past tell us we have to keep on pushing or we're not worth anything. That's not true. That's a lie to keep depression in control. I'm learning to schedule time for rest.

I had a friend share with me an observation about my life recently. He said, "You know, Will, when I think of all the things you've done in life, you've really done a lot." He went on to say, "Your life reminds me of an old pinball game. You know the one with the steel ball, and you pull the lever way back and let the ball fly. The ball bounces back and forth off of the bumpers." He went on to share how he saw my hands on the sides of the pinball machine pushing the flippers as fast as I could go to keep the ball moving.

His next statement was very telling. He said, "That has to be really tiring." Then he continued, "You know how the ball sometimes falls into a hole and stays there and all these points just keep racking up on the scoreboard?" I responded with a resounding, "Yes!" He said, "I think it's time for you to take your hands off the flipper and just sit in that hole and rest and let the points rack up." Now that's torpor.

Hummingbirds rely on torpor to survive the long cold nights. So many times I have wasted so much energy trying to get myself out of a place of discouragement and hopelessness rather than resting and waiting for the answer to come. God is faithful and will come through when we need Him. Sometimes fighting the situation makes it worse. "It's not by might, and it's not by power, but it's by My Spirit says the Lord" (Zechariah 4:6). It really is about God working in and through us to accomplish what He wants. Torpor in a way speaks of how we're called to yield to the will of God for our lives.

Torpor reminds me of Jonah in the Bible. God tells Jonah to go to a specific city with a message for the people of that city (Ninevah). But Jonah disobeys and goes the exact opposite direction. Truth is Jonah is angry with God because he knows God is going to show mercy on the city.

So Jonah jumps on a boat that's going in the opposite direction of Ninevah. While on this boat a storm comes, and the men on this boat confront Jonah. They decide to throw Jonah overboard. Jonah gets swallowed by a big fish and spends three days in the belly of this fish. (I'm so happy that God didn't choose that approach with me to get my attention.) Jonah is forced into a type of torpor as he spends time in the belly of this fish. Finally, the fish throws up Jonah onto dry land. Jonah ends up delivering the message to the people of Ninevah and all is well.

Think about it—three days or seventy-two hours in the belly of a fish. Now that's death. Dying can be a good thing if life comes out of it. When we're forced to die to self, then God can bring forth the good stuff, and that's what life is all about. It's not in material possessions, it's about coming to a place of rest, taking a deep breath and just knowing that at a particular moment all is well. I bet at some point during that seventy-two hours in the belly of the fish, Jonah just let go and realized there was no way out, so why fight it?

So many times God will put us in a place of torpor because He knows that's best for us. Going into deep sleep allows us to recover and rejuvenate ourselves so that we're ready for the next stage of life. This kind of rest can get us to where we want to be faster than spending all our energy and end up useless in the end.

Torpor is a state of almost lifelessness. Resting is being motionless—motionless not just physically, but mentally and spiritually—letting go and letting God, in a way. "Be still and know that I am God" (Psalm 46:10). What I have learned is that faith can be active while I'm resting. Faith tells me to rest and trust God is at work. I find peace in this concept, and it allows me to rest. The darkness would tell me that I need to be doing something or else I'm lazy, and on and on with the lies.

If I rest and let my faith be active, I can let go and not have to strive to make something happen. This keeps me in a place of trust. If I buy into the lie that I better get out there and make something happen, I risk spending my time and resources and end up in the same place anyway. My confidence ends up being in God alone.

The only real downside I see from torpor is that a hummingbird that is in a state of torpor is at risk from predators since they're in a state of lifelessness and can't be woken up with a nudge. The hummingbird is completely defenseless. A predator can come right in and take advantage. Sometimes when I'm trying to rest, thoughts will come to me, like, *Is this okay?* Or, *I really should be doing something*, or *this is a waste of valuable time*. Thoughts from "the predator" try to rip my joy away.

I was talking with my best friend Evan recently, and he shared an experience he had surfing. He was caught in a big storm and was drowning. As he told the story, he pointed to a diesel truck and said, "The white water alone was higher than that truck." He couldn't catch his breath and at one point hollered out, "I can't breathe!" At that moment a thought came to him, "But you can breathe right now." When he realized the truth of that fact, *at that moment he could breathe*, he said he totally relaxed.

He finished the story saying that once he relaxed, he just went with the waves and they ended up washing him to shore. The point to his story was that when he was panicking, his situation got worse. Once he was able to relax and go with the flow, he was brought to safety.

> At that moment a thought came to him, "But you can breathe right now."

It's another Sunday, and we just visited my friend Doug Webster's church, Lake Hills Community Church. Nan and I decided to stay close to home today and swing by and visit Doug's church. We go to his church maybe three or four times a year. What was interesting about this visit was the title of Doug's message, "Still Waters Run Deep."

He just happened to be preaching through the 23rd Psalm and was teaching on, "He leads me beside the still waters." He summed up his message with this formula: rest + refresh = restore. That's torpor! That's rest! Doug shared that sometimes God puts us into a forced rest. Couldn't have said it better myself. Torpor is a forced rest. Maybe, just maybe, that's why we're called to rest on the Sabbath, to force us to rest. Remember torpor is like a "slumber that is as deep as death." But then life comes forth.

Like in the case of Jonah virtually dead for three days in the belly of the fish, he goes to Nineveh and preaches, and life comes to a whole city. That's the hope I got from that little hummingbird. From death came life. When I gave it all up and couldn't do it anymore, God broke into my life set me free and life began. Maybe life begins at fifty-two?

Thanks; Hope, for teaching me about torpor. And thanks; Doug, for the confirmation that rest is an important part of the restorative process.

Lesson 18:

From Death to Life

*"I regret ever marrying you. I should've made that
decision with my head instead of my heart."*

— Nan Cuccia

THE DAY THAT Nan spoke those words was the day
I died to my marriage. I had to let my marriage go.
How could I blame her? The hell I put her through
merited every syllable in that statement—years of being left
alone through her own experience with a physical illness that
almost killed her.

Nan was ill for thirty-one months. Her body weight
dropped to ninety-four pounds. She had little energy to get
through the day. Day after day for thirty-one months, she was
locked up in her own cell abandoned by me. She had to learn
to deal with the resentment and anger growing daily in her
own life. My depression and rage had caused sin in her life.
How could she not be angry?

During those months that Nan suffered, I was away on business trips almost two weeks out of every month. I was racing around as fast as I could go to try to make up for lost time: trying to make it in the business world, trying to make a name for myself, trying to find an identity in my career. I was feeling angrier about each failed attempt to be successful, never realizing that the greatest failure was sitting right in my own home. I thought if I could just give Nan all the material things she would ever want, everything would be fine. She wasn't asking for anything. Nan was starving for a relationship.

I felt I couldn't give her what she wanted, and working hard became just another form of isolation. It allowed me to hide once again. Not under a car this time or under a bed. But I thought I could hide myself in my work, become successful, and then the depression and rage would be washed away by the success.

> I was feeling angrier about each failed attempt to be successful, never realizing that the greatest failure was sitting right in my own home.

After thirty-one months Nan was miraculously healed at a conference held at the River Vineyard, in Tustin, California. James Maloney was speaking on Friday and Saturday night. James has a worldwide healing and prophetic ministry. What's interesting about this man is that he had prophesied over Nan twenty-eight years earlier, telling her she would slay her Goliath like David did. A week before Nan got healed, her friend Diana sent her a card with a bag filled with five smooth stones. In the card were the words, "You will slay your Goliath like David."

Nan asked me if I would take her to the conference at the River Vineyard, and I reluctantly said yes. That evening as we were driving to the church, Nan kept saying that the name James Maloney sounded familiar to her. She shared the story of how a man had spoken a prophetic word over her some twenty-eight years ago, and she thought that his name was James Maloney.

> "You will slay your Goliath like David."

She continued to share that she remembered his wife's name was Joy. She wondered out loud *if this were the same man*. When James Maloney got up to speak that evening he introduced his wife Joy to the audience. Nan said *that's him*. I could hear her faith rise as the words came out of her mouth. That evening James Maloney prayed for Nan. It was real simple, not dramatic at all.

From where I was sitting I watched as James put his hand on Nan's head and said, "*Spirit of affliction, leave in Jesus' name.*" I watched Nan's head pull back and then rock forward. That was it. She came and sat back down. She shared with me on the way home that she saw this dark presence leave her head when her head went back. That was it. It's been almost two years now, and Nan has gained all her weight back and eats anything she wants. She works out whenever she wants (we walk four to six miles a night four nights a week). She's healed and living life with the same enthusiasm and more than she had before she got sick.

Nan had been healed for almost a year when we found Hope. Watching her nurse Hope and care for her with such compassion was no surprise. What she went through for those thirty-one months would cause most people to become embittered toward life or fall into the arms of God's compassion.

> That was it. She came and sat back down. She shared with me on the way home that she saw this dark presence leave her head when her head went back.

Thankfully Nan made the choice to take compassion and spend it on others. What makes my wife so successful in her business of caring for people through holistic medicine and herbs is her compassion. Knowing how people suffer with chronic illnesses firsthand is invaluable.

Nan chose to spend her compassion on Hope, and it paid off. She would get up in the middle of the night and check on that little bird. She was the one convinced that we had to take the bird home with us. She made one compassionate decision after another that allowed Hope to have a chance at life—not to mention me as well.

Nan had made the decision to divorce me and was making plans for a new life without the dysfunction of my rage and depression. Once she was healed, she realized that she didn't have to put up with the pain that my life brought her. I was unaware of what her plans were. She was living life basically as a single person cohabitating with me. She was compassionate and treated me just like she would any other person in her life.

She had severed the emotional ties of marriage and was moving on, though she never withdrew herself physically from me. Our sex life stayed intact, and that physical bond was an important connection. So many people withhold sex as a form of punishment, and that creates even more of a severing of the relationship.

Nan was waiting for just the right time, when one day she heard the fateful words that I believe saved our marriage. On that day she was making final plans to move on and start her new life, when in her spirit she heard the words, *just wait.* It was like God was giving her the option to wait. It wasn't a command but more of an option.

It was a free will choice to choose to wait. During that period of waiting she would hear God say that He makes all things beautiful in His time. She just wasn't sure of what God was making beautiful.

I don't think she was even sure at the time what she was waiting for. She was sure, though, that it wasn't me. She had already made her decision and was already investing time and emotions into her new life. A few months passed, and then that fateful morning came when I woke up and couldn't do life anymore. I was like Hope stuck in the grass and leaves, waiting for someone to help me.

In retrospect, the weeks that followed with Nan sharing in complete honesty her pain of what I had put her through brought the greatest healing. For the first time in my life I was able to listen without reacting in rage and hear the painful embarrassment I had caused her. For weeks we would stay up late, and she would share one embarrassing experience after another that my rage had caused her. Sometimes through her tears, I would just listen to the years that she spent covering up the awkward situations I had put her in, times when I had screamed out of control at some innocent person in public.

There were years and years of stories. I had no idea that all of this was in Nan and that it had created such a deep divide between us. Her love for me had died years ago. In the darkness of depression and rage, I thought we were living life together. I thought what we had was a normal healthy marriage. I had no idea how deep the river of dysfunction ran. The drowning effects it had on Nan were more than sobering to me.

Now our marriage is healthier than ever. What happened? Well, a lot of forgiveness and a lot of honest dialogue. We spent many evenings opening up to each other. Frankly, there has been a lot of letting go of expectations that we both put on each other. The healing that has taken place in our marriage has a lot to do with praying together and believing in God to rebuild trust. As time continues to pass, the healing process closes wounds that I thought could never be healed. Forgiveness and a willingness to be honest with each other go a long way in the hands of a loving God who's supporting our marriage.

In a daily practical way, marriage is about not competing with my wife to try and prove that I'm always right. We have disagreements, but what's important to me now is that I hear Nan and try to understand what she is saying from her heart. I don't have to be right. I can allow her to correct me without taking it personally, believing that she has my best interest in mind. This has allowed us to come together in different situations that arise rather than allowing them to create a wedge between us.

Marriage doesn't have to be hard. There doesn't have to be arguments that turn into angry outbursts that cause emotional damage to one another. No, unity in marriage can be achieved when two people are willing to love the other person above himself or herself. Yes, it takes time, but time is now on my side. As time passes, healing continues and love grows stronger. Trust is being rebuilt.

Is our marriage perfect? Of course not I mean, our marriage is already far beyond any dream I ever had when it comes to "happily ever after." Nan bought a sign that reads, "And they lived happily ever after." It hangs above the door that goes into our bedroom. I don't ever want to take that for granted.

I look forward each day for the opportunity to love God. After I take care of business with God in the morning, I look forward to loving my wife with my actions first and then my words. I look forward to loving others. I've devoted the rest of my life to investing my thoughts, time, resources, and energy in having the best marriage possible each day, one day at a time.

Days become weeks, weeks become months, and months will become years. I look forward to holidays together celebrating with all we have. One of the painful experiences Nan shared with me was how the rage and depression ripped off so many special occasions in our lives: Christmas, birthdays, holidays and special occasions in general.

My wife loves to celebrate. I mean *loves* to celebrate. She'll create ways to celebrate just for celebration's sake. Nan is full of joy and laughter; it's part of her nature. She gets that from her parents. Have you ever heard that slogan, "live, love, laugh"? That's Nan. My desire is to give her every opportunity to celebrate with joy and laughter. I love her laughter.

Life's so good without rage and depression. I've found what I've been looking for all my life. It's nothing grand in terms of career or accomplishments. When I hear Nan laughing on the phone or in her office with a client, that makes me happy. Becoming "a regular guy, just doin' happy" is my goal. And guess what happened? Nan and I went to Julian and got apple pie. We spent the entire day leisurely strolling through downtown, eating pie and ice cream, barbeque roast beef sandwiches, and cookies—you name it, we ate it.

And best of all, we bought each other new rings to celebrate the first day of fall and our new life together. I bought her a wonderful handcrafted green amethyst ring, and she bought me a handsome ancient Roman coin ring. We found a shady place under a tree and prayed blessings over each other as we placed the rings on our fingers, and then smooched for a while under that tree. Now that's doin' happy.

I've discovered that relationships are more valuable than accomplishments. I know some lonely people who have spent their entire lives stacking up "trophies of accomplishments" on their shelves, and they're still not happy. Spending my life on relationships—that's the lesson learned.

Lesson 19:

Hope's Eyes Revisited

Hummingbirds have very large eyes in proportion to their body weight. The eyes are set on the side of the head, allowing the hummingbird to see both ahead and on the side peripherally. Hummingbirds have many more rods and cones than humans in their eyes to help them see well. This makes them better able to see colors and ultraviolet light. Hummingbird eyes will regularly outweigh a hummingbird's brain.

Watch a young hummingbird in the nest long enough, and it's bound to look your way.

IT WAS TUESDAY, January 16, 1990. Nan looked my way, our eyes locked just for a moment, and my life was changed forever. That's the night that our eyes locked for the first time. This is the story of how we met. How we met, where we met, and the timing of when we met always encourages me when I tell this story. It's encouraging that God's in every detail of where we go and whom we meet.

I'd been living with my cousin in an apartment in the north part of the Orange County. My cousin was recently divorced, and I had been divorced for a little over two years. We thought of ourselves as the consummate bachelors. We were training for marathons, going out dancing and "living the life."

Nan was living about twenty miles south of me. She had been divorced for seven years and was in hot pursuit of God. She spent most of her free time going on dates to places by herself, spending her time with God. She called these "God dates."

As for me, on the other hand I was preaching the "gospel of Will" to all my buddies. I would tell my cousin, "We don't need women in our lives. All we need is Jesus." I was attending a small church at the time, and all the older women in the church were always trying to set me up on dates with their younger friends in the church. I would politely tell them that what I was looking for didn't exist. They would respond with, "What do you mean?" My retort was always the same, "I'm looking for a female Jesus."

Thank God for those women. It was one of those women who kept inviting me to a Bible study that was held at the Doubletree Hotel in Santa Ana off the Interstate 5 freeway. They would say that there was someone there they wanted me to meet. I put them off for about three months, until finally I just gave in knowing they would not relent.

On that Tuesday evening in January, Nan was home tucked in bed with her Bible and some chocolate chip cookies getting geared up for a nice quiet evening. Suddenly her phone rang, and on the other end was her good friend Diana. Diana was calling to invite Nan to a Bible study at the Doubletree Inn Hotel. Nan says that Diana bribed her by saying they could go out to dinner for pot roast before they went to the Bible study. Nan threw her jeans and a jacket on over her pajamas and headed out the door.

I was working for my uncle's construction company at the time and digging trenches for the most part. My job was to do anything my uncle wanted done, no matter how dirty or disgusting the job was. I got home from work that Tuesday afternoon and something very weird happened. I found myself getting all cleaned up, and I put on a suit and tie. Now, understand I hadn't worn a suit or tie for at least four years. I felt this excitement well up in me.

I had the thought that I was going to meet someone at that Bible study. Not a woman or wife, but someone who could help me get into ministry or at least get out of construction and do something more enjoyable. Or for that matter help me to do *what I was made to do*, whatever that meant. I arrived at the Bible study late, and the only seats that were available were in the front two rows. It was a little embarrassing to walk down the middle aisle after the study had started, especially in a suit and tie. Little did I know that arriving late was part of "the plan".

As I walked down the aisle, Nan was talking with Diana when she heard the words (in her mind), *Isn't that your husband?* She turned from Diana and looked as I walked by and sat down in the second row. All she saw was the back of my head. She just sat there and wondered what that was. What did she hear?

Sometime during the study, the woman who was teaching walked down the center aisle. As she walked by me, I turned around and that's when it happened. I can't explain it, but I would swear on my grandmother's grave as to what happened next. The entire room fogged over and all I could see was Nan's face. Everything else, I mean everything, was just foggy. I looked straight into her eyes, and our eyes locked. I quickly glanced at her left hand ring finger, which was resting on the chair in front of her, saw there was no ring, and then looked back to her eyes.

When the woman who was teaching walked back to the front, I turned around, totally dumbfounded. I just sat there. I didn't hear anything the rest of the evening. My first thought after I turned around was that Nan was my wife. I had this confidence rush though me that we were going to be married.

After the study was over, Nan and her friend left. Diana asked Nan who I was. Nan's response was, "How do I know? It's your Bible study. I've never been here before." Diana said, "Well, he sure seemed like he knew you." The next day Nan was leaving for Spain to do some design work for a client and was going to be gone for three months.

I drove home that evening in complete silence. My whole world was turned upside down with just one look from this "doe-eyed beauty." All I could think about was how much love was in her eyes. I would share with people later that all I saw that night was the love of Jesus in her eyes. I know it sounds so hokey, but I think God does have a sense of humor. It was like He was showing me that a "female Jesus" did exist, or at least that my views about being single was not part of His plan for my life.

I got home that evening and opened the door. There was my cousin watching the highlights on ESPN with his face buried in a bucket of Ben and Jerry's ice cream. He greeted me with, "What are you doing with a suit on?" I blurted out, "I think I met my wife." He responded back with, "Huh?" I went on to them him that I had gone to this Bible study, and I thought that I met my wife there. His questions accelerated, "What happened to 'We don't need women, all we need is Jesus'?" I said I knew that, and then just sat down on the sofa like I had been shot.

My cousin broke the silence with, "Well, what's her name?" I said, "I don't know." "You don't know," he echoed. I just shook my head. The next question was a typical guy question, "Well, is she pretty?" My response was, "I don't know." "You don't know?" he mimicked with disgust, and then with exasperation asked, "Does she have a good body?" I just shrugged my shoulders and softly answered, "I don't know." My cousin just stared at me for a moment turned off the television and silently strolled to his bedroom.

The next week passed slowly as I anticipated going to the Bible study in hopes of seeing Nan again. That next Tuesday came, and I got tied up at work and didn't make it to the study. The next three months passed, and I never made it back to the study. Every week that would pass I would make plans to go and something would come up.

Finally, I was able to return to the Bible study on Tuesday, April 24, which is Nan's birthday. Nan had returned from Spain the day before, and she had planned on going to the Bible study the next night. Her girlfriend Pam had called on Monday evening asking if she could take Nan out for her birthday. Nan responded with, "Yes, but can we go to a Bible study?" Pam inquired, "You want to go to a Bible study to celebrate your birthday?"

The next evening we both showed up at the study for the first time since our initial encounter. (What's interesting to me is that if I had gone back while Nan was in Spain, I might not have returned.) There were no seats available next to where Nan and Pam were sitting, so I chose a spot where I could check her out without being too obvious. Later, Nan would tell me that I was completely obvious about how I was checking her out. That evening we didn't talk, but Nan did say to Pam, "Do you see that cute guy over there?" Pam replied, "Yes." "I'm going to marry him," Nan proclaimed. Pam asked, "What's his name?" Nan answered with, "I don't know." "Well, I wouldn't marry him tomorrow," was Pam's response. Nan's confident proclamation was, "I won't."

I went home that evening excited that I had seen her again, but was disappointed with myself that I didn't have the courage to speak to her. I plotted my strategy for the next week. I decided that I would get to the study late and then just go sit next to her. I arrived late as planned and to my surprise Nan was not there. I panicked thinking that I may have missed my opportunity, and I would probably never see her again. Just as I was trying to decide if I wanted to stay or get up and leave. Nan walked in.

Slightly behind her was a guy who appeared to be with her. I thought what a fool I'd been and thank God I hadn't talked to her. They sat down together and just as I tried to catch a glance at Nan, she turned her back to the guy and winked at me. As I turned away to pretend I wasn't looking, I could feel my face flush red. I didn't know what to think.

Later Nan shared with me that "the wink" was her attempt to be sure that I knew she wasn't with that guy. They had walked into the hotel together, and when he saw that Nan was carrying a Bible he asked her if she was going to the Bible study and could she show him which room the study was.

Well, another week passed, and I still didn't speak to her. Frankly I wasn't sure what to think. I was sure she had winked at me, but I wasn't sure about the other guy. So I decided to wait another week. Actually I still lacked the courage to speak to her.

During those three weeks of silence Nan began to wonder if she had really heard God speaking at all. She had been married before and had no intentions of marrying again unless she was sure that God made it very clear to her whom it was that she was to marry. She thought, "God, if this is the man that you've brought for me to marry, why won't he even come up and say hello or introduce himself to me?"

Well, the next Tuesday rolled around and I was determined to speak to her. I had been beating myself up for being such a wimp. My cousin was chastising me as well. I arrived at the study primed with the confidence to just go up and speak to her. The study seemed to go on forever that evening, and as the night wore on my confidence began to waver. Finally the study ended, and I could feel my confidence evaporate as I stood up. I stalled until finally Nan left.

I followed her from a distance down the hall of the hotel until she walked out of the building. As I walked to my car, I was beating myself up that I had let another week slip away.

I got in my car and began to drive out of the parking lot when I realized that Nan was driving the car in front of me. Just as I recognized it was Nan, she pulled her car over and parked in front of the hotel.

Before I could think of what to do next, I found myself pulling over and parking behind her car. I waited for a moment to see if she were going to get out and go back in the hotel. She got out and did go into the hotel. I didn't know what to do. Should I follow her in? At that moment, she came out of the hotel and got back in her car. Without a thought, I got out of my car. I walked right up to the driver's side and tapped on her window.

She put her window down and looked at me with a big grin on her face that expressed clearly, "It's about time." I didn't have time to plan what I was going to say because I was still trying to figure out what the heck I was doing knocking on her car window. I said something stupid like, "Hi, I'm Will, and I've been wanting to meet you." I was so nervous that my lower lip was quivering. Now, understand it was late April, and it was a typical warm spring Southern California evening.

Nan laughed and responded with, "I'm Nan, are you cold?" I didn't know what to say so I just said, "Yes." She invited me to come sit in her car. I said, "Sure." We sat in her car and talked until almost midnight. I asked her if she were going to come to the Bible study next week and if so would she like to go out for coffee afterward? Nan said, "Yes." She said yes!

Nan actually asked me out on our first date the next week. She had been given tickets to a hot air balloon festival in Temecula from a guy from her church and instead of going with him she took the tickets and asked me to go with her. I think she realized that God needed help to kick start this relationship since I was so heavy footed. I was so excited to go. We met at five a.m. at a community college and took a tour bus down to the festival.

I waited five weeks before I held her hand, and Nan was continuing to question God about me. She couldn't figure out what was up with my lack of assertiveness. I just wanted to do things right and honor her. I was definitely attracted to her and was excited that if God had picked her for me, what a pick she was. I had been afraid that if I ever remarried, God would make me marry some dowdy frump for my penitence for living such a worldly life. *I know my view of God still needs some work.*

It was the end of May before I kissed her, and soon things became hot and heavy. We didn't want to sleep with each other before marriage. We wanted to honor God and each other. But it was at times difficult.

Lesson 20:

Rest and Wait

*Hummingbirds do not mate for life—the female raises
the young on her own. The male hummingbird is not
involved with raising the young.*

*"God made male and female to be together. Because of this, a
man leaves father and mother, and in marriage he becomes one
flesh with a woman—no longer two individuals, but forming
a new unity. Because God created this organic union of the two
sexes, no one should desecrate his art by cutting them apart."*

— Mark 10:5–9 The Message

*I've learned there is a difference between hummingbirds
and people. Hummingbirds don't mate for life. And even
though most marriages end in divorce, God intended
for marriage to be for life.*

NAN AND I decided that we would slow things down
until we were sure that God was leading us into
marriage. So we didn't see each other as much, but we

still talked on the phone late into the night. We were getting worn out physically and emotionally. We decided to take a week off from seeing each other and would meet at the Bible study at the hotel the next Tuesday.

It was a long week for me waiting to see her. I was sure that God had brought us together but wanted Nan to be sure. I prayed all week that God would speak to her. Tuesday came, and I got home from work and laid down to rest before the study that evening. Frankly I was emotionally exhausted. I had been resting for about twenty minutes when I had the thought that I was supposed to get Nan a stuffed animal for a present. What was peculiar about this thought was that Nan doesn't like stuffed animals.

I prayed and asked God if He was leading me to get Nan a stuffed animal. It was comical to me because Nan had shared numerous times that guys she had dated would always give her stuffed animals, and she made it clear that she didn't like them (the stuffed animal not the guys) and that I didn't have to waste any money on one for her. I really never planned on buying her a stuffed animal anyway, because I thought it would be a waste of money.

I began a humorous conversation with God about going to the mall and buying Nan a stuffed animal. I felt like God said, "Just trust Me, and I'll show you where to go and which stuffed animal to buy." It was like an exercise in faith. My thought was, *this sounds a bit ridiculous but I'll trust You.* When I got to the mall, I went straight to Nordstrom I didn't even know if they sold stuffed animals.

One of the salespeople directed me to the third floor. I spotted a cute little lamb and purchased it. As I walked out of the store I heard clearly the words, *that's not the one I wanted you to buy. You didn't even ask me.* I thought to myself, *this is silly.* I searched the entire mall, going in and out of stores quietly listening for God's leading. Time was getting short, and there was just enough time get back to the car and get to the Bible study.

I thought, *God, this is really kind of stupid, I trusted you but I must have been thinking this all up on my own.* Just as I was finishing that thought, I found myself walking down a mall corridor that was new and had just opened up. At the end of the corridor was a new gift shop. I walked in, and the salesperson behind the counter greeted me with, "Hello, can I help you?" Just as she completed her greeting, I looked up on the shelf behind her, and there it was, this huge stuffed lion just staring down at me.

Before I could return the greeting, I said out loud, "That's it!" The salesperson asked, "That's what?" "That big stuffed lion. I want that, that's it," I exclaimed to her. I knew that was the one. Nan had always called her previous boyfriends her "bear," but she said I was her "lion." I picked a card to go with it and wrote these words, "The lion's name is *RW,* short for Rest and Wait. This is your lion until God releases your real lion." I got a big gift bag and stuffed the lion into the bag. His head and shoulders hung out of the bag.

When I got to the hotel, my intention was to leave the lion in my car and then unveil it to Nan after the study was over in private. When I got out of my car, I heard the phrase; *I want you to take the lion with you.* I thought, *oh, come on now, not in front of all those people.* So I took RW into the Bible study with me. It was a real hit with all the women at the study. Nan just kept staring at RW and then at me.

That same Tuesday afternoon while I was chasing down the lion in the mall, Nan was having quite a different experience. She had been asking God to show her if I truly was her husband. She was driving through the canyon in Laguna Beach that afternoon and prayed, "God, if Will really is the *desire of my heart,* you've got to let me know tonight or I'm going to break this off."

That evening at the Bible study, the lady who was teaching the study walked up to Nan in the middle of the study pointed her finger at Nan and proclaimed, "Young lady God *h-a-s* given you the *desire of your heart*." And then she continued teaching.

I had no idea what had happened, but I could tell by Nan's reaction that those words were very significant to her. Nan was lost in her thoughts the rest of the evening. I could tell that she was there in body, but her mind was off somewhere else.

After the study Nan and I walked out to her car in silence as I lugged RW behind me. I could tell Nan was wondering what the heck I was doing with a big stuffed lion, and I could also tell she was still lost in her thoughts.

When we got to her car, I made a feeble attempt to justify why I bought her a stuffed animal, and then just decided to give her the card in hopes that the card would explain my intentions. As Nan read the card I couldn't hear a thing. It was complete silence. I didn't hear cars driving by in the parking lot or the traffic out on the street. I didn't hear the voices of the people as they walked by in conversation. It was silent. Then Nan responded with these words, "God has released my lion to me." I was stunned and clueless. I said, "What do you mean?" At that moment my heart was completely exposed. She went on to explain about her afternoon prayer and the specific way that it was answered.

We got in the back seat of her car and just stared at each other. I would say, "You're my wife," in utter amazement, and Nan would respond back with, "You're my husband." We must have said it a dozen times.

I proposed to her in August, and that is a story in itself. We had gone out to Long Beach on a date one evening. As we were walking on the wharf, we both felt this incredible warm sensation come over our chests and stomachs at the same time. It was early evening and quite cool and breezy. Our arms and legs and the air around us were cool, and we could feel the breeze on our arms and face, but our chests and stomachs were covered by a warm blaze.

At one point we looked at each other and said, "Do you feel that?" I know this may sound crazy, but it happened and no one could ever get me to deny it. God met us there and joined us together that evening. It was a supernatural experience. I believe that God knew how leery Nan was about entrusting her heart to anyone and how broken I was. This experience gave us an unwavering confidence that God was at work in bringing us together.

Because of that experience on the wharf that evening, I thought that would be the perfect spot to ask her to be my wife. At the wharf in Long Beach they have gondolas you can rent fully equipped with "gondola guy" striped shirt hat and sings, *the whole Venice gondola thing.* What better spot could there be for an Italian to ask his fiancée to be his wife?

That afternoon on the gondola I asked Nan to marry me. It happened again. For the entire forty-five minute ride on the gondola, everything was fogged out. All I could see was Nan, and all she could see was me. The ride seemed strangely short. God was joining us together. Not my depression, rage, nor anyone or anything could tear us apart.

Today, yes today, I am a regular guy "just doin' happy" with the most wonderful woman in the world. I'm excited about my life! God does do miracles. Today, God still heals the sick (both physical and emotional). Today, God still restores the brokenhearted. Today, God is still the God of hope. He is in the business of bringing life into situations that seem dead.

I'm not anything special. What I mean by that is in God's eyes you're every bit as important to Him. I'm just a regular guy. If God is truly excited about my life, I know He's excited about your life, too. Put your trust in Him *today* and see what happens.

Last Lesson

Hope Released, Faith Flies

The Portuguese call the hummingbird "beija-flor" or
flower-kisser.

"Rescue me from this prison, so I can praise your name.
And when your people notice your wonderful kindness
to me, they will rush to my side."
— Psalm 142:7 (Contemporary English Version)

I SAW FOUR HUMMINGBIRDS the other night as I walked around the lake in Mission Viejo. Nan said, "I wonder if any of those hummingbirds are Hope?" We both knew they weren't, but for as long as we live we will have Hope in our hearts. Every time we see a hummingbird or even hear the word hummingbird, we are reminded of Hope. Hope changed our lives forever.

The Portuguese call the hummingbird *beija-flor*, or flower-kisser. I will always feel the kiss of God's forgiveness every time I see a hummingbird. The thought that Hope is out flying free brings me joy, and my heart is flooded with thanksgiving. She's free to fly and be what she was always meant to be. I remember the week we spent feeding her with sugar water in a dropper. She would open her beak wide and just take in all she could from the dropper. She always seemed so desperate to be fed. She was restricted by our feeding schedule.

> She's free to fly and be what she was always meant to be.

Now she's free to fly and search for flowers to feed from in the way she was designed to do. In just one day she may visit 2,000 flowers for nourishment. Hope is now able to experience the adventure of life, searching, exploring her environment to find the spots that will become her places of nourishment.

Hope is free now from her cage to explore the possibilities of mating with another hummingbird. Just the thought of that makes me feel like a proud papa in some weird way. I wonder if Hope really is a girl or if she's a little male hummingbird. It doesn't matter. The thought that Hope is free to procreate is very cool. Maybe the grandbabies will call me papa Hope.

I do wonder if Hope is safe. She still faces danger every day. Other hummingbirds that are territorial could cause her danger. Other animals that are predators can put her in harm's way. Or even for that matter, those little red handles on the rope to an automatic garage door opener can be mistaken as a hummingbird feeder and present danger. She can be attracted to one of those red handles and get trapped in a garage. The truth is potential danger can be everywhere. Life is a risk.

That's where faith and trust take over. The dangers of freedom are worth it compared to being locked in a cage. I don't ever want to be imprisoned again. I know Hope doesn't either. That's why the moment she flew free and didn't return to her cage she became Faith.

Every day she must have faith that she will find flowers along her way. She must have faith that she will be safe from predators that could bring her harm and faith that even though she may not know what tomorrow brings, she'll be okay. She'll have food, a safe place to rest, and the hope of a new day.

Whether I call her Hope, or Faith, I've learned an important lesson in valuing today. I learned that time and money can't be my God. I can't look too far ahead. And I can't be ashamed of yesterday. Making the most of today and enjoying the beauty that comes from each day is more life giving than anything I can experience. Faith flies free today, spending time becoming what she was meant to be.

I guess this last lesson is not worrying about who I am or what I'll become. It's not about an identity, or a name. The truth is our little hummingbird is just what she was meant to be, a hummingbird. Her identity is not in her name whether we call her Hope or Faith. The lesson is simple. We helped set her free so she could be a hummingbird, a little creation of God that can fly like no other bird and pollinate from flower to flower. She can rest in torpor. She's a hummingbird.

I've spent half my life trying to figure out why I was created. Why was I put here on earth? And the answer was found in a week spent with a hummingbird. Live each day trusting that God will provide. Love God and love people. Do what's right in my heart to do each day. Know that God heals, and delivers when we need Him to.

This has been a story about a hummingbird and a regular guy becoming what they were meant to be. A hummingbird and a regular guy—how much more fulfilling can it get? The simple truth is that God cares. He does. I had a close friend tell me that he doesn't believe in God the way I do, but when he read this book (in manuscript form) it was the truth of the words that penetrated his heart that changed him.

My response is that if you pursue the truth, it will lead you to God. And when you find Him, truly find Him and know how real He can become in your life, you will become what you were meant to be.

I also know that people have a tough time believing that God can heal and deliver. Skepticism keeps people from experiencing the freedom that God is waiting to give. I know I was a skeptic. I thought *this is just the way I am. I'll never change. I just have to accept that I'll be taking medication for depression my entire life. I'll have to deal with the side effects that come with taking antidepressants.* Today I don't have to deal with any of these beliefs because God intervened in my life. It doesn't matter what people think, what matters is what God did.

There's a story about a man during the time of Jesus' ministry who lived in a tomb. He lived in isolation, alone and naked living in a cave. He lived outside of his town by the tombs. He lived alone because an unclean spirit, a demonic spirit, tormented him. The people of the town tried to restrain him with chains and shackles, but he couldn't be restrained. He'd snap the chains and smash the shackles.

Nothing was strong enough to restrain him. So he went out to the tombs to live in isolation. I'm sure he was afraid of what he might do to someone or even to himself. He spent day and night crying out among the tombs and in the mountains cutting himself with stones. I'm sure this behavior was his way of trying to self-medicate and deal with the pain that accompanied the torment.

Jesus came to this man's town one day. When the man saw Jesus coming from a distance he ran up to Jesus and knelt down. He cried out, "What do You have to do with me, Jesus Son of the Most High God?" He continued, "I beg You before God, don't torment me!"

Jesus simply said, "Come out of the man, you unclean spirit." Then Jesus asked the spirit, "What's your name?" "My name is Legion," he answered Jesus, "because we are many." Jesus then sent the unclean spirit into a nearby herd of pigs, and the pigs took off down the hill and jumped into a river and drowned.

The story gets better. The men who were herding the pigs ran off and started telling everyone in the town what had happened. Can you imagine? Everyone in town knew of the man who lived in the tombs. I'm sure everyone had a story they would tell about this "crazy" guy. Now these pig herders came to town with the most outlandish story of all. Jesus delivered the man. The spirits that lived in him jumped in the pigs, and the pigs took off into the river and drowned.

Jesus then showed up in town, and with him was the man who had been demon-possessed. This man was now dressed and in his right mind. That's right—the Bible says that the man was in *his right mind*. What's interesting about this story is the town people's reaction. They didn't know what to do with this guy or with Jesus. The man was healed and delivered, and the people were afraid of the results. They wanted Jesus to leave. I find this interesting. You'd think they'd all be excited and want Jesus to stay a while and maybe take care of some of their own issues. No, they want him to get on the first boat out of town. Some people just don't want their messes to become a message.

Jesus went down to the water. As he was getting into a boat to leave the town, the demon-possessed man who had been healed wanted to go with him. Jesus told him to go back to his town and share with the people what has happened to him. He went back and told everyone, and they were "amazed." Amazed was the people's response. When a life is changed people are amazed. I can see it now, the delivered man goes to town and people ask him, "Who are you?" And the man says, *I'm DELIVERED.*

Just yesterday Nan came home. Her response to me (even after all this time) was *I was driving home and realized I get to go home and be with my husband "who's normal, it's amazing."* I wanted to tell her, "I'd like to know how you define normal." The point is that God heals and delivers people, and as a result we are given a story to tell. Those stories cause the people listening to be amazed at what God does. God likes to take our messes and make a message. Real life stuff that's all messed up becomes what God uses to tell of the redemptive adventures that He likes to take us on.

I can relate to the demoniacs story really well. I know what it's like to be tormented by darkness. I know how it feels not to know of what you're capable. I know the fear that if rage takes over, there's no telling whom you might hurt. *If I just go and hide in the tomb I'll be safe.* I know those thoughts and feelings, the crying out day and night trying to understand what in the heck is wrong, trying to break free of the chains and shackles on my own strength. The weariness.

I know the constant torment of anxiety overwhelming me to the point of not being able to function. I'm not talking about an anxious thought. No, it's an anxiety that doesn't allow a person to function in the present moment. It keeps a person from being productive at work and in relationship, and it eventually leads to destruction. I'm talking about an anxiety that is debilitating and tormenting.

How does anxiety torment a person? Physically at times it would cause my stomach to be so upset, I would vomit. It would cause migraine headaches that would put me out of commission for an entire day or more. Worry, worry, and more worry. Eventually the body takes on that worry, and I would get sick. The anxiety then becomes fear.

There were so many times that I'd spend days in fear wondering when the next bout of anxiety would hit. I lived in fear that a migraine might hit if I make a wrong decision. Sometimes eating the wrong thing or stressing out over something or for that matter getting angry might bring on the next migraine. Shame and guilt would drive me to eat food for comfort that would contribute to more destruction to my body (a form of cutting myself with stones I guess).

Here's the vicious cycle I experienced. Anxiety would cause fear, fear would either cause me to isolate or withdraw, which would make me angry, or the fear would manifest itself with anger in a situation, and my anger would cause me to isolate. Either way it would lead me down the path of rage.

When rage would hit. I would then go into that dark place of depression that sometime lasted days. Whatever the cycle was, it would rip away the exciting life that God had intended for me and for those I loved as well. So I know the torment that the demoniac experienced.

More importantly, I know the reaction of the people. Sometimes I'll be in a situation sharing what God has done. How He just showed up, and for some reason it was my time. He answered the cry of my heart. He set me free. It's a look that people have that says, "That's nice, Will, but are you sure?" People have a tough time believing that God still does this stuff. Even people who are part of the Church, believers, have a tough time believing. I know I was the same way. But sometimes when a person listens to my story and it touches their life in a way that provokes a hunger for change in their own life it makes everything I've been through worth it.

The man who lived in the tombs begged Jesus to go with him when Jesus was getting in a boat to leave the man's town. But Jesus wouldn't let him go with him. He told him, "Go back home to your own people, and report to them how much the Lord has done for you and know He has had mercy on you" (Mark 5:19).

I'm going to spend the rest of my life doing just that: telling whomever I can that God delivered me and showed me mercy. I no longer take antidepressants. I'm free from the constant tormenting thoughts. Most days I spend enjoying life, and enjoying my wife. I'm excited about life.

Some will get excited with me as they hear my story, and hope will ignite inside them that maybe God could do the same for them or someone they love. And others tragically will choose, like the townspeople, to stay comfortable with whom they are, where they live and not have their lives interrupted by the crazy man who lived in the tombs. They'll say, "Just go away and leave us alone." I hope you choose to slow down and see what God will do for you; some may fall, but Hope flies.

I have always been a sucker for a happy ending to a movie or book. So now I will share my happy ending with you. Six weeks after we gave Hope to Lisa Birkle (Assistant Wildlife Director), of the Wetlands and Wildlife Care Center, specializing in the rescue, rehabilitation, and release of wild birds, Hope flew free. Lisa shared with Nan that Hope had been placed in a cage with five other hummingbirds. She told us that of the six birds in Hope's group, *he* (yes, we found out that Hope is a male hummingbird) was the strongest and was the first to take off out of the soft release cage and not return.

When Nan got off the phone, she said to me with tears in her eyes that see was so relieved that Hope made it okay. She went on to express that she had been concerned that when we hadn't heard from Lisa she was afraid that Hope had died. I joked and said, "So, Hope was valedictorian of his cage," but inside I was just as relieved to hear of his successful entry into his new world. In some strange way it brought a renewed confidence in all that I have learned from the experience of Hope coming into our lives. Yes, I can say with confidence that Hope flies free.

Epilogue

Nan gave me this article a few months after I started this manuscript. I thought this was a perfect way to close out the book and give people an idea of how misunderstood mental illness is in society. I'm proud that Nan shared this with me considering all the years she didn't agree with what this article says. It goes to show that people can change when God invades their life.

The following article was in the Mission Hospital magazine (fall issue 2008) called *My Health*. The title of the article is: "Abolish the Myths of Mental Illness." I've included this article to educate people who have family members or friends who suffer from depression. Be encouraged that even though this article states that depression is classified as a mental disorder that is a real illness that often requires medical treatment, remember God healed me of this disorder. God can do the same for anyone who trusts in Him to heal.

When it comes to talking about mental illness, people are often reluctant to share personal experiences or seek help. But staying silent is a dangerous game. By not seeking help, a mild disorder may spiral out of control.

How do we abolish the stigmas surrounding mental illness? Learn the facts. If you have been experiencing prolonged feelings of sadness and despair or have other mental health concerns, seek the help of a qualified professional and talk openly about what you are feeling. It's the first step toward getting the help you need to feel like yourself again.

MYTH: If I seek treatment, people will think I'm crazy.

FACT: Nearly two-thirds of people with a diagnosable and treatable mental disorder do not seek treatment out of fear of negative reactions. Remember that seeking medical treatment is a private matter between you and your care provider—and the first step toward making a full recovery.

MYTH: People with mental disorders are violent.

FACT: The majority of individuals with mental disorders are nonviolent. In fact, it's often hard to tell whether someone has a mental disorder unless you are a trained professional. About 57.7 million people in the U.S., nearly one in five, experience a diagnosable mental disorder every year.

MYTH: Mental disorders aren't medical by nature.

FACT: Mental disorders are real illnesses that often require medical treatment. In fact, many mental disorders are the result of chemical imbalances in the brain that can be treated with a combination of therapy and medication. For those who seek help, eighty to ninety percent see improvement.

MYTH: Kids don't have mental disorders; they are just acting out.

FACT: Mental disorders are a real problem that requires real treatment at every age. It is estimated that more than two million children and four out of 100 teenagers in the United States suffer from clinical depression.

MYTH: Mental illness is a weakness that can be willed away.

FACT: Mental Illness is a treatable condition that requires professional help. It can also have tragic consequences if left untreated. In 2004, more than 32,000 people took their own lives. It is estimated that thirty to seventy percent of those individuals were suffering from major depression or bipolar disorder.

As I just finished typing this article, Nan and I sat down to dinner. She brought up the question of what people would think about God's ability to do supernatural healing.

My response was simple; I told her that this is just my story of what God did for us. What people choose to believe and what God chooses to do in each situation may be different. All I know is that people have to believe God. God heals and delivers, and He still does it today. That's the message I will take with me wherever I go the rest of my life. Like I said before, "Some may fall, but Hope flies."

* * *

You can begin to fly today. It starts with this simple prayer: "Lord Jesus, I turn from my sins. I ask You to come into my heart. I make You my Lord and Savior." Then just simply begin to ask Him to deliver you from whatever keeps you captive. Ask God to bring the freedom that only He can give. I would love to hear from you if you prayed this prayer. You can reach me at regularguywill@yahoo.com. Nan and I would love to hear from you.

* * *

BRINGING HELP TO GHANA, WEST AFRICA

As part of an ongoing charitable initiative, Hands
Helping Hands a Non Profit Organization will
contribute One dollar from the purchase of this
book toward immune system building supplies to the
hospitals and other care facilities in Ghana that are
in desperate need of these supplies.
www.HopeBookToday.com

I invite you to visit my regular guy website and find
out what's available for the regular guys.
www.justdoinhappy.com

Made in the USA
Middletown, DE
21 October 2016